INNOVATION 101

A comprehensive introduction to some of the most important innovation concepts, models, theories, tools and techniques.

MARCH 17, 2024
TANVEER HUSSAIN

Contents

Preface		6
1.	**Historical Development of Innovation**	8
1.1	What is Innovation?	8
1.2	Evolution of Innovation Concepts	10
1.3	Examples of some Historic Innovations	13
1.4	Examples of Some Notable Innovators	17
1.5	Impact of Geopolitical Events on Innovation	19
2	**Theories of Innovations**	22
2.1	Schumpeter's Theory of Economic Development (1911)	23
2.2	Rogers' Diffusion of Innovations Theory (1962)	24
2.3	Kuhn's Structure of Scientific Revolutions (1962)	26
2.4	Tushman and Nadler's Organizational Frame Bending (1986)	27
2.5	Absorptive Capacity Theory (Cohen and Levinthal, 1990)	29
2.6	Christensen's Disruptive Innovation Theory (1997)	31
2.7	Blue Ocean Strategy (W. Chan Kim and Renée Mauborgne, 2004)	32
2.8	Multi-Level Perspective on System Innovation	34
3	**Dimensions of Innovation**	36
3.1	Profit Model	36
3.2	Network	38
3.3	Structure	40
3.4	Process	41
3.5	Product Performance	43
3.6	Product System	45
3.7	Service	46
3.8	Channel	48
3.9	Branding	49

	3.10	Customer Engagement	51
4		**Clayton Christensen's Typology of Innovations**	**53**
	4.1	Disruptive Innovation	53
	4.2	Sustaining Innovation	55
	4.3	Efficiency Innovation	56
	4.4	Comparative Analysis: Impact on Business Strategy and Growth	57
	4.5	Integration for Success: Blending Different Innovation Types	58
	4.6	Future Outlook: The Evolving Nature of Innovation	58
5		**Models of Innovation**	**60**
	5.1	Technology Push Model of Innovation (1950s)	60
	5.2	Market Pull Model of Innovation (1960s)	61
	5.3	The Coupling Model of Innovation (Rothwell, 1994)	63
	5.4	Four Dimension of Innovation Space	64
	5.5	Open Innovation Model (Chesbrough, 2003)	67
	5.6	Ten Types of Innovation (Doblin, 1990s)	68
	5.7	Lean Startup Methodology (Eric Ries, 2008)	70
	5.8	Gartner Hype Cycle in Innovation	71
	5.9	Technology Readiness Levels in Innovation	74
	5.10	The Golden Circle in Innovation	76
	5.11	Business Model Canvas (Osterwalder and Pigneur, 2010)	78
6		**Innovation Processes and Methodologies**	**80**
	6.1	Basic Research and Development (Early 20th Century Onwards)	80
	6.2	Brainstorming (1953)	81
	6.3	Brainwriting Ideation Technique	83
	6.4	Reverse Brainstorming Ideation Technique	85
	6.5	TRIZ (Theory of Inventive Problem Solving, 1956)	86
	6.6	Quality Circles Process for Innovation (1962)	88
	6.7	Idea Campaigns Ideation Technique	90

6.8	Broadcast Search Ideation Technique	91
6.9	SCAMPER Tool	93
6.10	Crazy 8 Ideation Technique	95
6.11	Pyramid Search Ideation Technique	96
6.12	LEGO Serious Play Ideation Technique	98
6.13	Nudging for Idea Generation	100
6.14	Voice of the Customer (VOC, 1980s)	102
6.15	Stage-Gate Process (Cooper, 1980s)	103
6.16	Agile Development (2001)	105
6.17	Design Thinking (2008)	107
6.18	Lean Canvas (2010)	109
6.19	Value Proposition Canvas (2012)	110
6.20	Crowdsourcing (Early 2000s Onwards)	112
6.21	Frugal Innovation (2010s)	114
7	**Popular Concepts and Notion about Innovation**	**116**
7.1	The Innovator's Dilemma	116
7.2	The 70-20-10 Rule of Innovation	118
7.3	The Three Horizon Innovation Framework	119
7.4	Jobs-to-be-Done	121
7.5	Build-Measure-Learn	123
7.6	Minimum Viable Product (MVP)	125
7.7	Prototyping	127
7.8	The Product Lifecycle Model	129
7.9	Lead User Method	130
7.10	A/B Testing	132
7.11	Stress Test	134
7.12	The Adoption Curve	136
7.13	The Chasm	138

7.14	Net Promoter Score (NPS)	139
7.15	Gartner Magic Quadrant	141
7.16	The Ansoff Matrix	143
7.17	The McKinsey Matrix	145
7.18	The BCG Matrix	147
7.19	Innovation Roadmap	149
7.20	The 4 U of Problems Worth Solving	151
7.21	The Eisenhower Matrix for Innovation Management	153
7.22	Project Triage	155
7.23	Transaction Cost Economics in the Context of Innovation	156
7.24	The Instrument Selection Framework	158
7.25	Value Co-Creation	159
7.26	Messaging Map	161
7.27	Customer Journey Mapping	162
7.28	Empathy Maps in Innovation	164
7.29	The Kano Model in Innovation	166
7.30	User Personas or Customer Personas	168
7.31	Morphological Analysis in Innovation	170
7.32	Six Thinking Hats in Innovation	172

Preface

Innovation is the cornerstone of progress, driving advancements that shape our future and redefine the boundaries of possibility. This book, *Innovation 101*, is crafted to serve as an essential guide for anyone eager to delve into the multifaceted world of innovation. Whether you are a student, an entrepreneur, a corporate leader, or simply an enthusiast, this text offers a thorough exploration of the principles, frameworks, and methodologies that underpin the dynamic process of innovation.

Our exploration begins with the historical development of innovation, tracing its evolution from ancient times to the modern era. We delve into seminal innovations that have transformed industries and society, from the invention of the printing press to the advent of digital photography. Each chapter not only highlights the technological advancements but also the visionary individuals behind them, offering insights into the minds that dared to challenge the status quo.

The theories of innovation provide a conceptual understanding of how and why innovation occurs. From Schumpeter's theory of economic development, which introduces the idea of creative destruction, to Christensen's disruptive innovation theory that explains how smaller companies can challenge established incumbents, this book covers a range of influential theories. These frameworks are essential for understanding the mechanisms of innovation and for applying them to real-world scenarios.

Innovation is not a monolithic concept but a spectrum of interrelated activities. The dimensions of innovation explored in this book, such as profit models, networks, structures, and processes, offer a granular view of how organizations can innovate across different aspects of their operations. We also examine various models of innovation, including the technology push and market pull models, and the more contemporary open innovation model proposed by Henry Chesbrough.

At the heart of innovation are the processes and methodologies that enable the generation and implementation of new ideas. From brainstorming and design thinking to lean startup methodologies and agile development, this book provides a comprehensive overview of the tools and techniques that drive innovation. These methodologies are presented with practical examples and case studies to illustrate their application in diverse contexts.

In today's fast-paced world, the ability to innovate is more crucial than ever. This book aims to equip readers with the knowledge and skills needed to navigate and lead in an environment where change is constant. By understanding the historical context, theoretical underpinnings, and practical applications of innovation, readers will be better prepared to foster a culture of innovation within their own organizations and beyond.

This book would not have been possible without the contributions of numerous scholars, practitioners, and thought leaders in the field of innovation. Their research, insights, and experiences have significantly enriched the content of this text. I am also deeply grateful to my colleagues, friends, and family for their unwavering support and encouragement throughout the writing process.

As you embark on this journey through the landscape of innovation, I hope you find inspiration and practical wisdom that empowers you to become a catalyst for change. Welcome to *Innovation 101*—let's explore the future together.

Tanveer Hussain
March 17, 2024

1. Historical Development of Innovation

In the realm of human achievement, innovation stands as a beacon of progress and a testament to the unyielding power of human curiosity and creativity. This chapter embarks on an enlightening journey through the annals of history, tracing the evolution of innovation from its earliest incarnations to its present-day manifestations.

1.1 What is Innovation?

Innovation is a term that carries multiple interpretations, each offering a unique lens through which to understand this dynamic and multifaceted concept. This section explores various definitions of innovation, providing a comprehensive view of what innovation entails across different contexts.

1.1.1 Classic Definition

Traditionally, innovation has been defined as the **process** of _generating new ideas and successfully implementing_ them. This involves not just the creation of new ideas or concepts but also the practical application and adoption of these ideas in a way that significantly alters a domain or sector. Innovation constitutes not merely a novel idea, but it comprises a novel idea plus its successful implementation.

1.1.2 Business and Economic Perspective

In a business context, innovation is often seen as the **process** of _creating new products, processes or services_ or _improving the existing_ products, processes or services. Economically, it can be viewed as a key driver of growth, competitiveness, and productivity, often measured by factors like the number of patents filed or the introduction of new products in the market.

1.1.3 Technological Innovation

From a technological standpoint, innovation is frequently associated with the **process** of _developing new technologies_ or the _applying existing technologies in a novel way_ to create new products, processes or services. This could range from groundbreaking inventions to incremental improvements that enhance performance or efficiency.

1.1.4 Social Innovation

Social innovation refers to **process** *of developing and implementing new strategies, concepts, ideas, and organizations to solve a social problem or meet a social need* – e.g. from working conditions and education to community development and health - and that extend and strengthen civil society. This perspective emphasizes the impact of innovation on societal well-being and social structures.

1.1.5 Sustainable Innovation

Sustainable innovation focuses on *creating processes, products, and solutions that are not only economically viable but also environmentally friendly and socially equitable.* It's increasingly important in the context of global environmental challenges and the push for more sustainable business practices.

In conclusion, innovation can be viewed through various lenses, each providing a distinct understanding of its nature and impact. Whether it's transforming industries, driving economic growth, addressing societal challenges, or pushing the boundaries of technology, innovation remains a key element in shaping the future and driving progress.

1.1.6 Process vs. Product Innovation

- Process Innovation: Involves the implementation of a new or significantly improved production or delivery method. This includes significant changes in techniques, equipment, and/or software.

- Product Innovation: Involves the introduction of a good or service that is new or substantially improved. This might include improvements in technical specifications, components and materials, software, user friendliness, or other functional characteristics.

1.1.7 Open vs. Closed Innovation

- Open Innovation: A paradigm that assumes firms can and should use external ideas as well as internal ideas, and internal and external paths to market, as they look to advance their technology.

- Closed Innovation: Refers to processes that limit the use and development of innovations to internal teams and structures, typically within a single company or entity.

1.1.8 Radical vs. Incremental Innovation
- Radical Innovation: Introduces a fundamental change, often creating a new market or disrupting an existing one. It's associated with high risk but potentially high reward.
- Incremental Innovation: Small improvements or upgrades to existing products, services, processes, or methods that maintain or enhance competitiveness.

1.2 EVOLUTION OF INNOVATION CONCEPTS

The concept of innovation has undergone a significant transformation over the centuries, evolving from an often negatively perceived notion to a key driver of economic, social, and technological progress.

1.2.1 Ancient Origins

The journey begins in the ancient world, where innovation was often driven by survival and practical needs. Early humans innovated primarily in the realms of tool-making, agriculture, and shelter construction. These were not labeled as 'innovations' in their time but were essential adaptations to their environment. In ancient civilizations like Egypt, Mesopotamia, and the Indus Valley, innovation was closely tied to the development of writing systems, monumental architecture, and urban planning. These innovations were often driven by the needs of the society, such as efficient farming techniques, water management, and the establishment of governance systems.

1.2.2 The Classical and Medieval Insights

Moving into the classical and medieval periods, innovation began to take on a more structured form. The Greeks and Romans contributed significantly to the fields of science, mathematics, and engineering. Innovations from this era include the development of the aqueducts, the refinement of surgical techniques, and the foundations of modern philosophy and scientific inquiry.

The medieval period saw the amalgamation of Eastern and Western knowledge, particularly during the Islamic Golden Age. Innovations in navigation, medicine, and mathematics were significant during this time. The invention of the printing press in the 15th century by Johannes Gutenberg was a pivotal moment, as it democratized knowledge and set the stage for the Renaissance and the subsequent scientific revolution.

1.2.3 Early Views on Innovation (17th-19th Century):

- Initial Perceptions: In its earliest conceptions, particularly during the 17th and 18th centuries, 'innovation' was viewed with skepticism and fear. It was often equated with political and social upheaval, seen as a threat to established norms and traditions.

- Industrial Revolution: The 19th century's Industrial Revolution marked a turning point. Innovation began to be associated with positive societal change, linked to the marvels of machinery, industrialization, and technological breakthroughs. It became synonymous with progress, efficiency, and economic growth.

1.2.4 Schumpeter and the Idea of Creative Destruction (Early 20th Century):

- Schumpeter's Influence: Economist Joseph Schumpeter revolutionized the understanding of innovation in economics. He viewed it not just as a process of incremental improvements but as a radical force of transformation.

- Creative Destruction: Schumpeter's concept of 'creative destruction' described how new innovations often render existing technologies, skills, and arrangements obsolete, paving the way for new economic structures and progress.

1.2.5 Post World War II Expansion (Mid 20th Century):

- Innovation in the Cold War Era: Post WWII, particularly during the Cold War, innovation became a linchpin for national security and economic dominance. It was an era marked by the Space Race, nuclear advancements, and significant technological competition between superpowers.

- R&D and Technological Advancements: There was substantial investment in research and development, leading to breakthroughs in electronics, computing, healthcare, and materials science.

1.2.6 The Rise of Innovation Management (Late 20th Century):
- Systematic Study of Innovation: Pioneers like Peter Drucker began to study innovation systematically, introducing it as a critical discipline within business management.
- Innovation as a Manageable Process: The realization that innovation could be cultivated and managed within organizations led to the development of new business strategies and models focused on fostering innovative thinking and practices.

1.2.7 Disruptive Innovation and Beyond (1990s Onwards):
- Clayton Christensen's Theory: The 1990s introduced the groundbreaking concept of **'disruptive innovation'** by Clayton Christensen [1]. It highlighted how smaller, more agile companies could upend established businesses by leveraging new technologies and innovative business models.
- Strategic Advantage of Innovation: This period underscored the importance of innovation as a strategic tool for competitiveness and growth, shifting the focus to understanding its dynamics in the business landscape.

1.2.8 Open Innovation (Early 21st Century):
- Henry Chesbrough's Open Innovation: The concept of **'Open Innovation'** proposed by Henry Chesbrough[2] marked a paradigm shift. It suggested that companies should not only rely on internal ideas but also incorporate external innovations and collaborations.
- Collaborative Approaches: This led to more networked, collaborative approaches to innovation, integrating external partnerships and crowd-sourced solutions into traditional R&D processes.

1.2.9 Digital and Technological Innovation (21st Century):
- Digital Revolution: The ongoing digital revolution, marked by advancements in AI, blockchain, and the Internet of Things (IoT), has drastically changed the innovation landscape, emphasizing digital transformation.

---

[1] https://claytonchristensen.com/
[2] https://haas.berkeley.edu/faculty/chesbrough-henry/

- Focus on User Experience: Current innovation strategies focus heavily on enhancing user experience and leveraging data analytics for more personalized, efficient solutions.

1.2.10 Social Innovation and Sustainability (21st Century):
- Addressing Global Challenges: Innovation is increasingly directed towards addressing pressing global challenges like climate change, poverty, and health crises.
- Sustainable Technologies and Social Enterprises: This includes the development of sustainable technologies, social entrepreneurship, and innovative approaches to create a more equitable and sustainable world.

Throughout its history, the concept of innovation has changed from being perceived as a sporadic and disruptive event to being recognized as a continuous, manageable process integral to economic, societal, and technological advancement. This evolution reflects the increasing complexity and interconnectedness of challenges faced by modern societies, positioning innovation as a crucial tool for future progress and sustainability.

1.3 Examples of some Historic Innovations

The history of innovation is marked by numerous groundbreaking inventions that have not only transformed industries but also significantly impacted society and daily life. Here is an expanded look at some of these historic innovations, presented in chronological order:

1.3.1 The Printing Press (Information and Publishing) - 15th Century:
- Innovation: Johannes Gutenberg's invention in the mid-15th century mechanized the process of transferring text and images to paper.
- Impact: This innovation democratized knowledge, making books and printed materials more *accessible* and breaking the monopoly of the educated elite over information.
- Outcome: It played a pivotal role in the Renaissance, the Reformation, the Age of Enlightenment, and the scientific revolution, fundamentally altering the course of human history.

1.3.2 Wright Brothers' First Flight (Aviation) – 1903:
- Innovation: Orville and Wilbur Wright achieved the first powered, sustained, and controlled airplane flight in 1903.
- Impact: This marked the birth of modern aviation, a significant leap in transportation technology.
- Outcome: It transformed global travel, increasing the *speed of travel* across continents, and had profound effects on warfare, commerce, and international relations.

1.3.3 Ford Model T (Automobile Industry) – 1908:
- Innovation: Henry Ford introduced the first *affordable* automobile for the average American in 1908.
- Impact: Revolutionized transportation and American industry through the introduction of mass production techniques, notably the assembly line.
- Outcome: Cars became *accessible* to the masses, fundamentally changing the way people lived and worked and spurring growth in related industries like oil and rubber.

1.3.4 Penicillin (Medical Field) – 1928:
- Innovation: Discovered by Alexander Fleming and later mass-produced, penicillin was the first true antibiotic.
- Impact: This marked the beginning of the antibiotic era, drastically reducing deaths from bacterial infections.
- Outcome: Transformed medical treatment, significantly extended life expectancy, and paved the way for further medical breakthroughs in treating infectious diseases.

1.3.5 The Internet (Global Communication and Information Sharing) – 1960s Onwards:
- Innovation: Developed from the 1960s, with milestones like the creation of ARPANET and the World Wide Web by Tim Berners-Lee.
- Impact: Revolutionized the way information is shared and accessed, leading to the digital age.

- Outcome: Altered every aspect of daily life, from communication to commerce, education, and entertainment, connecting the world in unprecedented ways.

1.3.6 Apple iPhone (Telecommunications and Technology) - 2007:
- Innovation: Launched in 2007, it combined a phone, internet browser, and music player into a single device with a touchscreen interface.
- Impact: Transformed the smartphone market, setting new standards for mobile computing and user interface design.
- Outcome: Spurred the growth of the app economy, changed the way people communicate, and significantly impacted various industries, from retail to media.

1.3.7 Blockchain Technology (Digital Transactions and Cryptocurrency) - 2008:
- Innovation: Initially conceptualized by an individual (or group) known as Satoshi Nakamoto for the digital currency Bitcoin.
- Impact: Introduced a decentralized ledger system, providing a new way of securing digital transactions without the need for centralized authority.
- Outcome: Has potential implications far beyond cryptocurrencies, including in areas like supply chain management, digital identity verification, and secure voting systems.

1.3.8 CRISPR-Cas9 (Biotechnology) - Early 2010s:
- Innovation: The development of CRISPR-Cas9, a groundbreaking gene-editing technology, by scientists Jennifer Doudna and Emmanuelle Charpentier.
- Impact: Revolutionized the field of genetics by allowing precise, directed changes to DNA, which was previously a complex and less accurate process.
- Outcome: Has significant potential in treating genetic disorders, improving crop resilience, and advancing our understanding of human biology.

1.3.9 Electric Vehicles (Automotive Industry) – 2010s Onwards:

- Innovation: The rapid advancement and adoption of electric vehicles (EVs), led by companies like Tesla.
- Impact: A major step towards reducing carbon emissions in the transportation sector, challenging the traditional internal combustion engine's dominance.
- Outcome: Spurred a global shift in the automotive industry, with major manufacturers committing to electric futures and the development of EV infrastructure.

1.3.10 5G Technology (Telecommunications) – Late 2010s:

- Innovation: The rollout of 5G networks, offering significantly higher speeds and lower latency compared to previous generations of mobile networks.
- Impact: Enhances mobile connectivity and is a key enabler for emerging technologies like the Internet of Things (IoT), augmented reality (AR), and autonomous vehicles.
- Outcome: Expected to transform various sectors including healthcare, manufacturing, and urban planning through improved connectivity and data handling.

1.3.11 Artificial Intelligence Advancements (Various Fields) – 2010s–2023:

- Innovation: Significant strides in artificial intelligence (AI), particularly in areas like machine learning, natural language processing, and computer vision.
- Impact: AI has become integral in various applications, from predictive analytics and personalized medicine to autonomous systems and content creation.
- Outcome: Continues to redefine industries, raising questions about the future of work, ethics in AI, and the balance between automation and human input.

1.3.12 Quantum Computing (Computing and Information Technology) - Early 2020s:

- Innovation: Progress in developing quantum computers, which use quantum bits (qubits) to vastly outperform traditional computers in certain tasks.

- Impact: Promises to revolutionize fields like cryptography, material science, and complex system simulation.

- Outcome: Still in early stages, but the potential applications of quantum computing could lead to breakthroughs in drug discovery, financial modeling, and climate research.

1.3.13 Renewable Energy Technologies (Energy Sector) - 2010s-2023:

- Innovation: Advancements in renewable energy technologies, particularly in solar photovoltaics, wind energy, and battery storage.

- Impact: Essential for the transition to a more sustainable energy system, reducing dependence on fossil fuels and mitigating climate change.

- Outcome: Increasing adoption globally, driving down costs, and leading to innovations in energy storage and grid management.

These case studies represent the cutting edge of innovation as of 2023, showcasing how new technologies continue to reshape industries, redefine societal norms, and address some of the most pressing challenges of our time. The pace and impact of these innovations underscore the ever-evolving nature of technology and its profound influence on the world.

1.4 EXAMPLES OF SOME NOTABLE INNOVATORS

The chronicles of innovation are replete with individuals whose vision and determination have profoundly reshaped our world. The following list offers a chronological look at some of these remarkable figures:

1.4.1 Al-Khwarizmi (c. 780-850) - Persian Mathematician and Astronomer:

- Al-Khwarizmi's work in mathematics, particularly his book on algebra, was foundational in the development of this field. He is often referred to as the "father of algebra," and his works introduced the decimal positional number system to the Western world.

1.4.2 Ibn Al-Haytham (965-1040) - Arab Mathematician, Astronomer, and Physicist:
- Known as the father of modern optics, Ibn Al-Haytham made significant contributions to the principles of optics and visual perception. His Book of Optics is considered one of the most influential books in the history of physics.

1.4.3 Thomas Edison (1847-1931) - Inventor and Businessman:
- Credited with developing many devices in fields such as electric power generation, mass communication, sound recording, and motion pictures, including the electric light bulb.

1.4.4 Nikola Tesla (1856-1943) - Inventor and Electrical Engineer:
- A pioneer in the development of alternating current (AC) electrical systems and electromagnetic technology, leading to the second industrial revolution.

1.4.5 Marie Curie (1867-1934) - Physicist and Chemist:
- The first woman to win a Nobel Prize and the only person to win in two different scientific fields, known for her discovery of radium and polonium.

1.4.6 Ada Lovelace (1815-1852) - Mathematician and Writer:
- Often regarded as the first computer programmer for her work on Charles Babbage's Analytical Engine.

1.4.7 Rosalind Franklin (1920-1958) - Chemist and X-ray Crystallographer:
- Her work on X-ray diffraction images of DNA was critical in understanding the DNA double helix structure.

1.4.8 Steve Jobs (1955-2011) - Co-founder of Apple Inc.:
- Known for his significant contributions to consumer electronics with products like the Apple II, Macintosh, iPod, iPhone, and iPad.

1.4.9 Tim Berners-Lee (1955-present) - Computer Scientist:
- Inventor of the World Wide Web, revolutionizing information sharing and access.

1.4.10 Elon Musk (1971-present) - Entrepreneur and Business Magnate:
- Known for founding and leading companies like SpaceX, Tesla, Inc., Neuralink, and The Boring Company, contributing to the electric car industry and commercial space travel.

1.4.11 Jeff Bezos (1964-present) - Entrepreneur and Media Proprietor:
- Founder of Amazon.com, he transformed an online bookstore into a powerful retail and technology giant.

1.4.12 Mark Zuckerberg (1984-present) - Media Magnate and Internet Entrepreneur:
- Co-founder of Facebook, pivotal in the rise of social media and its global impact on communication and advertising.

Each of these innovators, in their unique way, has not only contributed to their respective fields but also altered the very fabric of how we live, work, and perceive the world around us. From ancient scholars who laid the foundational bricks of modern science to contemporary entrepreneurs redefining the digital landscape, their collective legacies continue to inspire and drive progress across the globe.

1.5 Impact of Geopolitical Events on Innovation

The impact of geopolitical events on innovation is a profound and multifaceted phenomenon. Throughout history, major events such as wars, economic shifts, and political upheavals have often acted as catalysts for technological and scientific breakthroughs. These events create unique challenges and needs, which in turn drive societies and individuals to innovate.

1.5.1 Wars and Military Conflicts:
- **World Wars**: The World Wars were periods of intense technological and scientific innovation. World War I saw the development of technologies such as tanks, chemical warfare, and improved medical treatments. World War II accelerated advancements in radar, jet engines, nuclear technology, and computing. For example, the development of the

atomic bomb under the Manhattan Project and the creation of the first digital computers like the Colossus and the ENIAC were direct outcomes of the wartime need for advanced weaponry and rapid, complex calculations.

- **Cold War**: The Cold War era spurred a race for technological supremacy, most notably in space technology and arms. The space race led to significant advancements in rocketry, satellites, and eventually led to the moon landing. It also accelerated the development of technologies that have civilian applications, like satellite communication and GPS.

1.5.2 Economic Shifts:

- **Industrial Revolution**: The Industrial Revolution was both a result of and a catalyst for innovation. It began as a response to economic needs such as increased production and efficiency and led to the development of steam power, mechanization of production, and the factory system.

- **Globalization**: The rise of globalization in the late 20th and early 21st centuries has spurred innovation in communication technologies, logistics, and supply chain management, driven by the need for efficient global trade and communication.

1.5.3 Political and Social Movements:

- **Environmental Movement**: The rise of environmental consciousness and political movements focusing on sustainability have led to innovations in renewable energy technologies, electric vehicles, and sustainable manufacturing practices.

- **Digital Rights and Privacy**: In response to concerns over privacy and digital rights, there has been innovation in encryption, cybersecurity, and blockchain technology.

1.5.4 Public Health Crises:

- **Medical Innovations**: Epidemics and pandemics, like the HIV/AIDS crisis and the COVID-19 pandemic, have fast-tracked innovations in medical research, vaccine development, and public health strategies. The rapid development of mRNA vaccines for COVID-19 is a notable example.

1.5.5 Economic Crises:

- **Great Depression and Recession**: Significant economic downturns like the Great Depression and the 2008 financial crisis have often led to new financial regulations, economic theories, and innovations in economic policy and practices.

In essence, geopolitical events often create urgent, specific needs or open up new opportunities, driving societies and individuals to innovate. These innovations often have lasting impacts, extending far beyond the resolution of the events that spurred their development. They not only address immediate challenges but also lead to long-term advancements and shifts in various fields, ranging from technology and medicine to economics and social practices.

2 Theories of Innovations

Some scholars make a distinction between innovation theories and innovation models, although they are closely related and often intertwined.

Innovation Theories:

- Theories are explanations of how and why innovation occurs. They provide a conceptual understanding of the processes and dynamics of innovation. Theories are often developed through research and observation and aim to explain underlying principles.

- For example, Schumpeter's Theory of Economic Development explains innovation as a driver of economic change through 'creative destruction', and Rogers' Diffusion of Innovations Theory explains how, why, and at what rate new ideas spread through cultures.

Innovation Models:

- Models are frameworks or tools used to apply innovation theories in practical settings. They offer structured ways to approach and manage the innovation process within organizations or systems. Models can be prescriptive, offering steps to follow, or descriptive, providing a way to understand how innovation processes work.

- For instance, the Stage-Gate Process is a model that outlines a series of steps for developing and launching new products. The Open Innovation Model, proposed by Henry Chesbrough, is a framework for understanding and implementing innovation strategies that incorporate external ideas and pathways alongside internal ones.

In essence, theories provide the "why" of innovation, offering explanations and understanding, while models provide the "how," offering practical frameworks and guidelines for implementing innovation. Both are essential for comprehensively understanding and effectively executing innovation in various contexts.

2.1 Schumpeter's Theory of Economic Development (1911)

Joseph Schumpeter, an Austrian-American economist and political scientist, introduced his groundbreaking Theory of Economic Development in 1911. This theory, a cornerstone of innovation studies, profoundly impacted our understanding of the dynamics of economic change, particularly the role of innovation and the entrepreneur in capitalist economies.

2.1.1 Core Concepts of Schumpeter's Theory:

- **Innovation as the Driver of Economic Change**: Schumpeter posited that economic development is driven primarily by innovation. He identified innovation as *new combinations of existing resources*, which could take the form of new products, new methods of production, new markets, new sources of supply, or new organizational structures.

- **The Role of the Entrepreneur**: Central to his theory is the figure of the entrepreneur, whom Schumpeter saw as the catalyst for innovation. The entrepreneur disrupts the equilibrium of the existing economic order by introducing innovations, leading to what Schumpeter famously termed as "creative destruction."

- **Creative Destruction**: This concept is perhaps the most influential aspect of Schumpeter's theory. It refers to the process of transformation that accompanies radical innovation. Old industries are destroyed and replaced by new industries, just as new products replace outdated ones. This relentless cycle of destruction and creation is what drives economic growth and advancement.

2.1.2 Implications of Schumpeter's Theory:

- **Economic Cycles**: Schumpeter's theory implies that capitalist economies are characterized by cyclical fluctuations, largely due to the uneven pace at which innovations are introduced and diffused.

- **Capitalist Evolution**: Schumpeter's view of capitalism is dynamic and evolutionary, constantly being reshaped by technological innovations and the entrepreneurial activities that bring them to market.

- **Policy and Strategy**: For businesses and policymakers, the theory underscores the importance of fostering innovation and entrepreneurship. It also highlights the inevitability of change and the need for adaptability in the face of transformative innovations.

Schumpeter's Legacy: Schumpeter's Theory of Economic Development laid the groundwork for numerous subsequent theories and models of innovation. It shifted the focus from static economic models to a more dynamic view where change and innovation are central. His emphasis on the disruptive nature of innovation and the role of the entrepreneur has resonated across generations, influencing both academic thought and practical business strategies.

Schumpeter's theory remains highly relevant in today's fast-paced and technology-driven global economy. Understanding his concepts helps to appreciate the forces behind economic growth and the transformative power of innovation. It provides a framework for analyzing how new technologies and business models can disrupt established industries and create new economic opportunities.

2.2 Rogers' Diffusion of Innovations Theory (1962)

Everett M. Rogers, a prominent American communication theorist and sociologist, introduced the Diffusion of Innovations Theory in his 1962 book, "Diffusion of Innovations." This theory explores how, why, and at what rate new ideas and technology spread through cultures. Rogers' work has been influential in fields ranging from marketing and development studies to health promotion and technology adoption.

2.2.1 Key Elements of Rogers' Diffusion Theory:

- **Innovation**: Rogers defines innovation as an idea, practice, or object perceived as new by an individual or other unit of adoption.
- **Communication Channels**: The means by which information about the innovation is transmitted to members of a social system.
- **Time**: The process of adoption over time is typically illustrated in Rogers' famous S-curve. It describes the rate at which an innovation is adopted by members of a social system.
- **Social System**: The group of individuals who together adopt the innovation.

2.2.2 Stages of the Adoption Process:

Rogers outlines five stages through which an individual typically progresses in the decision process of adopting or rejecting a new innovation:

1. **Knowledge**: The individual is first exposed to the innovation and gains some understanding of its use.

2. **Persuasion**: The individual forms a favorable or unfavorable attitude towards the innovation.

3. **Decision**: The individual engages in activities that lead to a choice to adopt or reject the innovation.

4. **Implementation**: The individual puts the innovation into use.

5. **Confirmation**: The individual seeks reinforcement for the innovation decision made and may change if exposed to conflicting messages about the innovation.

2.2.3 Adopter Categories:

Rogers classifies adopters into five categories based on their readiness to adopt new innovations:

1. **Innovators**: Venturesome and eager to try new ideas.

2. **Early Adopters**: Respected leaders in social systems, slightly more cautious than innovators.

3. **Early Majority**: Deliberate before adopting new ideas.

4. **Late Majority**: Skeptical and adopt innovations only after a majority in their social system have done so.

5. **Laggards**: Last to adopt an innovation, based on tradition and past experiences.

2.2.4 Factors Affecting the Rate of Adoption:

The rate at which an innovation spreads is influenced by factors such as:

- Relative Advantage: The degree to which an innovation is perceived as better than the idea it supersedes.

- Compatibility: How consistent the innovation is with the values, experiences, and needs of potential adopters.

- Complexity: How difficult the innovation is to understand and use.

- Trialability: The extent to which an innovation can be experimented with on a limited basis.
- Observability: The extent to which the results of an innovation are visible to others.

Rogers' Diffusion of Innovations Theory provides valuable insights into the mechanisms and challenges of spreading new ideas and technologies. Its relevance extends beyond academic theory, offering practical guidance for businesses, policymakers, and social change advocates seeking to promote new innovations in society.

2.3 Kuhn's Structure of Scientific Revolutions (1962)

In 1962, Thomas Kuhn, a physicist, historian, and philosopher of science, published a seminal work titled "The Structure of Scientific Revolutions." His theory challenged the then-prevailing view of science as a steady, cumulative acquisition of knowledge and instead proposed that transformative innovations (or scientific revolutions) cause paradigm shifts in scientific disciplines.

2.3.1 Paradigm Shifts in Science:
- **Normal Science**: Kuhn introduced the concept of "normal science," which is the regular work of scientists theorizing, observing, and experimenting within a set of accepted beliefs and values, known as a "paradigm."
- **Anomalies and Crisis**: When anomalies or unexplainable occurrences challenge the existing paradigm, and the scientific community can no longer ignore these anomalies, a crisis occurs.
- **Scientific Revolutions**: These crises lead to periods of revolutionary science, where old paradigms are replaced with new ones. This process is not smooth or continuous but involves radical shifts in understanding and perspective, which Kuhn termed "paradigm shifts."
- **New Paradigm**: Once a new paradigm is accepted, it becomes the new basis for normal science, leading to another cycle of normal science under the new set of beliefs.

2.3.2 Applications Beyond Science:

While Kuhn's work focused on scientific disciplines, his concept of paradigm shifts has been influential in understanding innovation in various fields, including technology, economics, and social sciences. It provides a framework for understanding how fundamental changes occur in any field of human endeavor.

2.3.3 Examples of Paradigm Shifts:

- **The Copernican Revolution**: The shift from the Ptolemaic geocentric universe to the Copernican heliocentric model is an example of a scientific revolution that fundamentally changed the field of astronomy.

- **The Theory of Relativity**: Einstein's theory altered the scientific community's understanding of space, time, and gravity, replacing Newtonian mechanics under certain conditions.

2.3.4 Kuhn's Impact on Innovation Studies:

- **Non-linear Progress**: Kuhn's theory implies that progress in any field isn't a linear path but a series of disruptions and shifts that dramatically change the landscape.

- **Resistance to Change**: It acknowledges the resistance to change and the difficulty of paradigm shifts, as existing beliefs and systems are deeply entrenched.

- **Collaborative Innovation**: Kuhn's emphasis on the role of the scientific community in paradigm shifts highlights the importance of collaboration and collective effort in innovation.

Thomas Kuhn's "The Structure of Scientific Revolutions" offers a profound understanding of the dynamics of change and innovation. It underscores that major advances, whether in science or other domains, often require overturning established norms and thinking, leading to new perspectives and paradigms. Kuhn's work continues to inspire and inform those who study and participate in the processes of innovation and change.

2.4 TUSHMAN AND NADLER'S ORGANIZATIONAL FRAME BENDING (1986)

In 1986, Michael Tushman and David Nadler introduced the concept of "Organizational Frame Bending," a significant addition to the discourse on organizational change and innovation. This theory was developed as a response to the challenges organizations face in adapting to environmental shifts while maintaining operational efficiency.

2.4.1 Understanding Frame Bending:
- **Concept**: Frame bending refers to significant yet incremental changes an organization makes in response to external pressures and internal misalignments. It is less radical than a complete overhaul (or frame breaking) but more substantial than routine adjustments.
- **Objective**: The primary aim of frame bending is to realign the organization's structure, strategy, and processes with its changing environment without disrupting its core operations.

2.4.2 Key Elements of Frame Bending:
- **Balancing Stability and Change**: Tushman and Nadler's model emphasizes the importance of maintaining a balance between the stability of core processes and the need for change to remain competitive.
- **Incremental Change**: Unlike disruptive or radical innovation, frame bending involves making thoughtful, measured adjustments to an organization's structure and processes.
- **Leadership Role**: Effective leadership is critical in frame bending, as leaders must recognize when change is necessary and skillfully guide the organization through the transition.

2.4.3 Applications in Business:
- **Adapting to Market Shifts**: Organizations use frame bending when adapting to gradual market shifts, technological advancements, or changes in consumer behavior.
- **Restructuring for Efficiency**: Implementing new technologies or restructuring departments to improve efficiency are examples of frame bending.

2.4.4 Examples of Frame Bending:
- **Technology Adoption**: A company gradually implementing a new IT system to improve communication and data management without disrupting its day-to-day operations.
- **Organizational Restructuring**: A corporation shifting its organizational structure from a hierarchical to a more flat and flexible model to foster better communication and quicker decision-making.

2.4.5 Implications for Management:
- **Navigating Change**: Managers must be adept at identifying when incremental changes are needed and effectively implementing these changes without causing undue disruption.
- **Cultural Considerations**: Successfully bending the frame often requires a supportive culture that is open to change and continuous improvement.

Tushman and Nadler's concept of Organizational Frame Bending offers a pragmatic approach to organizational change. It recognizes the need for continuous adaptation and improvement in a dynamic business environment while also acknowledging the importance of maintaining operational stability. This theory provides a valuable framework for leaders and managers to navigate the complexities of change in a structured yet flexible manner.

2.5 ABSORPTIVE CAPACITY THEORY (COHEN AND LEVINTHAL, 1990)

In 1990, Wesley Cohen and Daniel Levinthal introduced the Absorptive Capacity Theory in their seminal paper, "Absorptive Capacity: A New Perspective on Learning and Innovation." This theory has since become a cornerstone in the study of organizational learning and innovation.

2.5.1 Core Concept of Absorptive Capacity:
- **Definition**: Absorptive capacity is defined as the ability of a firm to recognize the value of new external information, assimilate it, and apply it to commercial ends. It is not just the ability to acquire information but also to internalize and utilize it effectively.
- **Components**: Absorptive capacity is comprised of three key components: the ability to identify and understand potentially valuable

new knowledge (acquisition), the ability to assimilate this knowledge (assimilation), and the ability to apply or exploit this knowledge to create new knowledge and commercial outputs (exploitation).

2.5.2 The Role of Prior Knowledge:

- **Importance of Prior Knowledge**: Cohen and Levinthal stressed that a firm's ability to evaluate and utilize external knowledge is largely a function of the level of prior related knowledge it possesses. This includes not only basic skills and training but also a firm's structure, routines, and procedures.

- **Continuous Learning**: The theory highlights the importance of continuous learning and knowledge development within an organization to maintain and enhance its absorptive capacity.

2.5.3 Applications in Innovation Management:

- **Innovation Strategy**: Firms with high absorptive capacity are better positioned to innovate as they can effectively leverage external research and development.

- **Collaborations and Partnerships**: Companies with greater absorptive capacity benefit more from alliances and partnerships, as they can more effectively utilize external knowledge and expertise.

2.5.4 Examples and Implications:

- **R&D Investments**: Companies like Pfizer and Google invest heavily in R&D not only to develop new products but also to maintain their absorptive capacity, ensuring that they remain at the forefront of innovation in their industries.

- **Academic-Industry Partnerships**: Universities and research institutions often collaborate with industry partners, but the success of these collaborations hinges on the industry partner's ability to absorb and apply the new knowledge.

Absorptive Capacity Theory provides valuable insights into how companies can enhance their innovative capabilities. It underscores the importance of not only acquiring new knowledge but also effectively integrating it into the organization's operations and strategy. For businesses looking to innovate and stay competitive, investing in building and maintaining absorptive capacity is crucial.

2.6 Christensen's Disruptive Innovation Theory (1997)

Clayton M. Christensen, a renowned Harvard Business School professor, introduced the Disruptive Innovation Theory in his 1997 book, "The Innovator's Dilemma." This theory has been instrumental in understanding how small companies with fewer resources can successfully challenge established incumbents in a market.

2.6.1 Defining Disruptive Innovation:

- **Disruptive vs. Sustaining Innovation**: Christensen differentiated between 'disruptive' and 'sustaining' innovations. Sustaining innovations are incremental improvements to existing products or services, while disruptive innovations create entirely new markets and value networks, eventually displacing existing market leaders.

- **Characteristics of Disruptive Innovations**: Typically, disruptive innovations start in a niche market that may initially seem unattractive or inconsequential to established firms. These innovations often offer simpler, cheaper, more accessible, or more convenient alternatives to existing products.

2.6.2 Mechanism of Market Disruption:

- **Initially Underestimated by Incumbents**: Large, established companies often overlook the potential of disruptive innovations because they focus on improving their products for high-end or more profitable customer segments.

- **Gradual Market Penetration**: Disruptive innovations gradually move upmarket as they improve, eventually capturing the more demanding segments of the market and overtaking incumbent firms.

2.6.3 Examples of Disruptive Innovation:

- **Digital Photography vs. Film Photography**: Digital cameras were initially inferior in quality to film cameras but eventually improved and became widely accessible, leading to the downfall of major film photography companies.

- **Streaming Services vs. Traditional Media**: Streaming services like Netflix disrupted the traditional media and entertainment industry by offering a convenient and affordable alternative to cable television and movie rentals.

2.6.4 Implications for Business Strategy:
- **Recognizing Disruption**: Companies need to be aware of the potential for disruptive innovations in their industry and consider strategies to either compete with or adopt these innovations.
- **Investing in Innovation**: Christensen suggests that established companies should set up autonomous divisions tasked with exploring and developing disruptive innovations.

Christensen's Disruptive Innovation Theory has significantly influenced how businesses approach innovation and competition. It highlights the importance of being vigilant in the face of emerging technologies and market shifts, and the need for agility and adaptability in business strategy. This theory remains highly relevant in the rapidly changing landscape of modern industries.

2.7 BLUE OCEAN STRATEGY (W. CHAN KIM AND RENÉE MAUBORGNE, 2004)

Developed by W. Chan Kim and Renée Mauborgne in their 2004 book titled "Blue Ocean Strategy," this concept challenges traditional competitive strategy models. Instead of battling competitors in existing markets, or "Red Oceans," businesses are encouraged to create new, uncontested market spaces, termed "Blue Oceans."

2.7.1 Conceptual Framework of Blue Ocean Strategy:
- **Creating Uncontested Market Space**: Blue Ocean Strategy is about breaking away from competition and creating a new market space where the competition is irrelevant.
- **Value Innovation**: The cornerstone of Blue Ocean Strategy is value innovation. This involves creating powerful leaps in value both for the company and its customers, thereby opening up new and uncontested market space.
- **Eliminate-Reduce-Raise-Create Grid**: A tool used in this strategy to reconstruct market elements in crafting a new value curve. The idea is

to eliminate and reduce the factors an industry competes on and raise and create elements that the industry has never offered.

2.7.2 Principles of Blue Ocean Strategy:

1. **Reconstruct Market Boundaries**: Challenging conventional industry boundaries and exploring new possibilities.

2. **Focus on the Big Picture, Not the Numbers**: Concentrating on the overall strategy canvas and not getting bogged down by numbers and existing competition.

3. **Reach Beyond Existing Demand**: Instead of focusing only on existing customers, explore ways to tap into non-customers.

4. **Get the Strategic Sequence Right**: Ensure that the business model is commercially viable and the idea can be executed effectively in the market.

2.7.3 Examples of Blue Ocean Strategy:

- **Cirque du Soleil**: By blending opera and ballet with the circus format while eliminating star performers and animal shows, Cirque du Soleil created a new genre of entertainment.

- **Nintendo Wii**: Nintendo didn't try to compete with PlayStation or Xbox for the same customers. Instead, it created a new market with the Wii, targeting families and casual gamers with motion-sensing technology.

2.7.4 Implications for Businesses:

- **Innovation and Growth**: Blue Ocean Strategy pushes companies to innovate and grow by exploring new opportunities and creating demand, rather than fighting over a shrinking profit pool.

- **Strategic Thinking**: It requires a shift in perspective from competition-focused strategic thinking to a focus on value innovation and exploring new market potential.

Blue Ocean Strategy provides a significant shift in business strategy, emphasizing the creation of new markets and the capture of new demand. It offers a framework for businesses to think creatively about their market position and opportunities for innovation, encouraging them to venture beyond conventional boundaries and tap into new areas of growth.

2.8 Multi-Level Perspective on System Innovation

The Multi-Level Perspective (MLP) on system innovation is a framework for understanding long-term transformative change in complex systems. Developed within the field of sustainability transitions research, MLP provides insights into how large-scale changes occur in societal systems, such as energy, transportation, or healthcare.

2.8.1 Key Components of MLP:

MLP views transitions as interactions between three analytical levels:

1. **Niche Innovations (Micro Level)**: This level represents the space where radical innovations emerge. These are often small-scale, initially nurtured in protected environments like incubators or research labs, and can potentially disrupt existing systems.

2. **Socio-Technical Regimes (Meso Level)**: This level includes the dominant practices, rules, technologies, and networks that stabilize existing systems. The regime is resistant to change due to lock-in and vested interests.

3. **Socio-Technical Landscape (Macro Level)**: The broadest level, encompassing overarching political, cultural, and economic factors that shape and are shaped by regimes and niches. Changes at this level are slow-moving but can create windows of opportunity for niche innovations.

2.8.2 Dynamics of Change in MLP:

- **From Niche to Regime**: For a transition to occur, niche innovations must grow and link together, eventually challenging and potentially replacing the dominant regime.

- **Landscape Pressures**: Changes at the landscape level, such as economic crises or demographic shifts, can create pressures on the regime, leading to opportunities for niche innovations to break through.

- **Co-evolution and Alignment**: Successful transitions often require alignment and co-evolution between elements at all three levels.

2.8.3 Applications of MLP:

- **Sustainability Transitions**: MLP has been widely used to analyze historical transitions in energy systems, such as the shift from coal to renewable energy sources, and to inform policy for future sustainability transitions.

- **Innovation Policy**: The framework is used to understand how policy can support emerging innovations and facilitate their scaling and integration into existing systems.

2.8.4 Examples of System Innovation via MLP:

- **Electric Mobility**: The emergence of electric vehicles can be seen as a niche innovation. Changes in environmental policies and shifting cultural attitudes towards sustainability are landscape factors that can enable this niche to challenge the petrol-based automotive regime.

2.8.5 Implications for Businesses and Policymakers:

- **Strategic Niche Management**: Businesses and policymakers can use MLP to strategically manage and support niche innovations, understanding the broader context in which these innovations must operate.

- **Anticipating Change**: MLP helps in anticipating how broader socio-technical changes might impact industries and in identifying emerging opportunities.

The Multi-Level Perspective offers a comprehensive framework for understanding systemic innovation and transition. By considering the interactions between niches, regimes, and landscapes, MLP provides valuable insights for businesses, innovators, and policymakers aiming to drive or adapt to transformative changes in complex systems.

3 Dimensions of Innovation

Doblin, a global innovation firm, has outlined ten different dimensions of innovation that can help businesses improve their products, services, and overall strategies. Here's an explanation of each dimension:

3.1 Profit Model

This dimension focuses on the way a company makes money. It involves innovating the revenue streams, pricing mechanisms, and cost structures. Following are different profit model innovation tactics:

1. **Premium**: Selling products or services at a higher price point due to perceived value, exclusivity, or quality. Example: Luxury brands like Rolex or Louis Vuitton charge premium prices for their high-quality, exclusive products.

2. **Cost Leadership**: Offering products or services at the lowest cost to become the preferred choice for price-sensitive customers. Example: Walmart uses its massive scale to offer lower prices than competitors.

3. **Scaled Transactions**: Leveraging the ability to conduct large volumes of transactions, often with a small margin, to generate profit. Example: Credit card companies like Visa process a high volume of transactions and make money on small fees from each.

4. **Microtransactions**: Small financial transactions, often used in digital services and games. Example: Mobile games that offer in-game currency or special items for small amounts of real money.

5. **Forced Scarcity**: Deliberately limiting supply to increase demand and pricing. Example: Supreme releases limited quantities of new products, creating a sense of urgency and exclusivity.

6. **Subscription**: Charging a recurring fee for continued access to a product or service. Example: Netflix charges a monthly subscription fee for unlimited streaming of TV shows and movies.

7. **Membership**: Similar to subscription, but often includes a sense of belonging to a club or group. Example: Costco charges an annual

membership fee, giving customers access to bulk goods at discounted rates.

8. **Installed Base**: Profiting from a large installed base of users by selling them additional products, services, or upgrades. Example: Apple's large user base of iPhone owners who are likely to purchase apps, music, and services.

9. **Switchboard**: Connecting different sides of a platform and taking a fee for the matchmaking service. Example: Uber connects drivers with passengers and takes a percentage of the fare.

10. **Auction**: Selling products or services to the highest bidder. Example: eBay allows sellers to list items for auction, with the platform taking a cut of the final sale price.

11. **User-Defined**: Allowing users to set the price they're willing to pay. Example: Humble Bundle lets customers pay what they want for bundles of video games.

12. **Freemium**: Offering a basic product or service for free while charging for premium features. Example: LinkedIn offers free professional networking, with the option to pay for additional features like InMail or advanced search.

13. **Flexible Pricing**: Adjusting prices based on demand, customer segment, or other variables. Example: Airlines use dynamic pricing to adjust ticket prices based on demand and timing.

14. **Float**: Earning interest on money that's held temporarily. Example: Insurance companies invest premiums collected and earn interest before paying out claims.

15. **Financing**: Offering credit to customers to facilitate purchases. Example: Car manufacturers like Ford offer financing options to customers buying new vehicles.

16. **Ad-Supported**: Providing products or services for free, supported by advertising revenue. Example: Google offers its search engine for free, supported by advertising.

17. **Licensing**: Allowing others to use your intellectual property in exchange for a fee. Example: Microsoft licenses its Windows operating system to PC manufacturers.

18. **Metered Use**: Charging based on the amount of product or service used. Example: Utility companies charge customers based on the amount of water, gas, or electricity consumed.

19. **Bundled Pricing**: Selling a group of products or services together at a single price. Example: Cable companies offer bundles of television, internet, and phone services.

20. **Disaggregate Pricing**: Separating out parts of a product or service that were traditionally bundled and charging separately. Example: Airlines now often charge separately for checked baggage, seat selection, and meals.

21. **Risk Sharing**: Partnering with other companies to share the risk of new ventures. Example: Pharmaceutical companies sometimes partner to share the costs and risks of drug development.

Each of these tactics can be employed to carve out a unique position in the market and generate revenue in innovative ways, depending on the company's business model, industry, and customer base.

3.2 NETWORK

Innovations in this area involve how a company connects with others to create value. It can include partnerships, alliances, and other forms of collaboration. Leveraging networks can help a company expand its reach, share costs, and enhance its offerings through the strengths of others. Following are different network innovation tactics:

1. **Merger/Acquisition**: This involves combining with or purchasing another company to acquire its capabilities, products, or market access. Example: Disney's acquisition of Pixar allowed it to leverage Pixar's animation expertise and storytelling capabilities.

2. **Consolidation**: Similar to mergers and acquisitions, consolidation involves combining multiple entities within an industry to streamline operations and reduce competition. Example: The consolidation of

airlines like United and Continental to improve route efficiency and cut costs.

3. **Open Innovation**: This is the practice of sourcing ideas, insights, and technologies from outside the organization to drive innovation. Example: Procter & Gamble's "Connect + Develop" initiative partners with external entities to co-create new products.

4. **Secondary Markets**: Creating or tapping into a market for the trade of goods and services that were not part of the original business model. Example: Tesla has built a secondary market for its used electric vehicles, offering certified pre-owned cars.

5. **Supply Chain Integration**: Streamlining the supply chain to create efficiencies, often through technological integration or strategic partnerships. Example: Zara uses advanced supply chain management to rapidly respond to fashion trends and shorten production cycles.

6. **Complementary Partnering**: Collaborating with businesses that offer complementary products or services. Example: Spotify partners with various hardware companies like Bose and Sonos to ensure their service is easily accessible across different devices.

7. **Alliances**: Forming strategic partnerships to work toward common goals while remaining independent organizations. Example: Star Alliance, a global airline network, allows airlines to offer customers more destinations through a shared network.

8. **Franchising**: Allowing individuals or entities to operate a business under your brand and business model. Example: McDonald's franchises allow for rapid global expansion with reduced capital expenditure for the parent company.

9. **Coopetition**: Competitors working together on projects or in areas where they do not directly compete. Example: Samsung and Apple, despite being competitors in the smartphone market, collaborate with Samsung providing components for Apple's devices.

10. **Collaboration**: Working with other organizations, possibly from different sectors, to innovate or improve services. Example: Google

collaborating with NASA to work on research projects using Google's quantum computers.

Each of these tactics involves leveraging relationships and networks outside of the traditional boundaries of the firm to innovate and create value. They can lead to new growth opportunities, improved efficiency, and greater market reach.

3.3 STRUCTURE

This pertains to the organizational setup, including the physical and virtual infrastructure, employee hierarchy, and asset distribution. Innovating in this area can involve restructuring the organization for greater efficiency, flexibility, or employee empowerment. Each of the following structural innovation tactics involves changes to the internal architecture of an organization, impacting how it operates and competes in the marketplace:

1. **Organizational Design**: Refers to the way an organization structures its internal processes and hierarchies to optimize performance and adaptability. Example: Valve Corporation operates with a flat organizational structure, where there are no traditional managers, and employees are encouraged to join projects that interest them.

2. **Incentive Systems**: These are mechanisms put in place to motivate and encourage desired behaviors from employees. Example: Google uses a variety of incentive systems, including bonuses and '20% time'—where employees can spend 20% of their time working on projects they're passionate about.

3. **IT Integration**: Involves the use of technology to streamline processes and improve communication within an organization. Example: FedEx uses integrated IT systems to track packages, manage logistics, and optimize delivery routes in real-time.

4. **Competency Center**: A centralized department or team within an organization that focuses on a specific area of expertise, providing support and sharing knowledge across the company. Example: Siemens has established various Competence Centers focusing on areas like automation, digitalization, and electrification to support its global operations.

5. **Outsourcing**: Contracting out certain business processes or functions to external firms to reduce costs or focus on core competencies. Example: Alibaba outsources its website maintenance and customer service to third parties, allowing it to scale rapidly without major investments in these areas.

6. **Corporate University**: An educational entity within a company that provides training and development tailored to the organization's needs. Example: McDonald's Hamburger University trains and develops franchise owners and corporate managers in business operations and leadership.

7. **Decentralized Management**: Shifting decision-making power from a central executive team to individual business units or teams. Example: Toyota is known for its decentralized management approach, where frontline workers have the authority to stop production lines if they detect a problem, emphasizing quality and responsiveness.

8. **Knowledge Management**: The practice of collecting, distributing, and effectively using knowledge within an organization. Example: Accenture has a comprehensive knowledge management system that stores project insights, best practices, and expertise to be shared across the firm globally.

9. **Asset Standardization**: Establishing common standards for assets to ensure compatibility, reduce costs, and simplify maintenance. Example: SAP uses standardization of its software assets to ensure that its products can easily integrate with a wide variety of systems and technologies.

Each of these tactics can improve efficiency, productivity, and innovation within an organization, shaping not just the internal workings of the company but also how it interacts with the market and its customers.

3.4 Process

This dimension involves the methods and procedures companies use to do their work. Innovating processes can lead to more efficient, cost-effective, or higher-quality output. It might include implementing new technologies, adopting lean manufacturing techniques, or streamlining operations. Let's look at each of the process innovation tactics and provide examples of how they can be applied:

1. **Process Standardization**: Implementing uniform procedures to ensure consistency and efficiency. Example: McDonald's standardizes its food preparation processes across all outlets to ensure that customers receive the same quality of food regardless of location.

2. **Localization**: Adapting processes to meet the needs of different markets or regions. Example: Coca-Cola adjusts its product recipes in different countries to cater to local tastes and preferences.

3. **Process Efficiency**: Streamlining processes to reduce waste and increase productivity. Example: Toyota's implementation of the "Toyota Production System" is focused on continuous improvement and the elimination of waste, which significantly increases efficiency.

4. **Flexible Manufacturing**: Creating manufacturing processes that can be quickly altered to respond to changes in demand or customization requests. Example: BMW uses flexible manufacturing systems that allow it to customize cars based on individual customer preferences without slowing down production.

5. **Process Automation**: Using technology to automate tasks that were previously done manually to increase speed and reduce errors. Example: Amazon uses robots in its warehouses to automate the picking and packing processes, which speeds up order fulfillment and reduces the chance of human error.

6. **Crowdsourcing**: Leveraging a large group of people, usually from the online community, to generate ideas or solve problems. Example: LEGO uses its Ideas platform to crowdsource ideas for new toy sets from its fan community.

7. **On-Demand Production**: Producing goods only when there is a demand to reduce inventory costs and waste. Example: Zara's fast-fashion model relies on on-demand production to quickly bring new designs to market based on real-time fashion trends.

8. **Lean Production**: Minimizing waste within manufacturing systems without sacrificing productivity. Example: Dell's build-to-order system

where computers are built only when an order is placed, reducing inventory costs and waste.

9. **Logistics Systems**: Innovating in the coordination of complex operations involving the movement of goods. Example: UPS uses advanced logistics systems to optimize delivery routes and manage shipments efficiently across the globe.

10. **Strategic Design**: Planning and executing processes with strategic objectives in mind, often incorporating design thinking principles. Example: IDEO helps organizations redesign their processes with a human-centered approach, often leading to breakthrough innovations.

11. **Intellectual Property**: Using patents, copyrights, and trademarks to protect and manage innovations. Example: Pharmaceutical companies protect new drug formulas with patents, which allows them to profit from their research and development investments.

12. **User Generated**: Utilizing content or solutions created by end-users for the benefit of the product or service. Example: YouTube allows users to create and upload their own videos, generating a vast library of diverse content without traditional production costs.

13. **Predictive Analytics**: Using data, statistical algorithms, and machine learning techniques to identify the likelihood of future outcomes based on historical data. Example: Netflix uses predictive analytics to recommend movies and TV shows to users based on their viewing history.

Each of these tactics enables organizations to refine and evolve their processes, often leading to increased competitiveness, better customer experiences, and the capability to rapidly adapt to new market demands or technological changes.

3.5 PRODUCT PERFORMANCE

This focuses on the features and functionality of the product itself. Innovation can occur in product design, usability, quality, or new features that meet evolving customer needs. It's about enhancing the core offerings to differentiate from competitors. Product performance innovation involves tactics that enhance the value proposition of a product through its features, design, and functionality:

1. **Superior Product**: Creating a product that is best in class in terms of quality and performance. Example: The iPhone is often cited as a superior product due to its build quality, ecosystem, and user experience.

2. **Ease of Use**: Designing products that are intuitive and simple for consumers to use. Example: Dyson's vacuum cleaners are designed with ergonomic considerations and straightforward functionality to simplify the user experience.

3. **Engaging Functionality**: Incorporating features that make the product enjoyable and engaging to use. Example: Video game consoles like the Nintendo Switch offer unique interactive experiences through innovative controllers and gameplay.

4. **Safety**: Enhancing the safety features of a product to protect users. Example: Volvo's automobiles have a long-standing reputation for incorporating advanced safety features that exceed industry standards.

5. **Feature Aggregation**: Combining multiple features or functions into one product. Example: Smartphones today aggregate the functionality of a camera, GPS, computer, and phone into one handheld device.

6. **Added Functionality**: Introducing new features to a product to provide additional benefits. Example: Smartwatches now often include health monitoring features such as heart rate sensors and oxygen saturation detectors.

7. **Performance Simplification**: Removing unnecessary complexity from a product to improve its core performance. Example: The Google search engine stands out for its simple interface and quick, relevant search results, despite the complex algorithms operating behind the scenes.

8. **Environmental Sensitivity**: Designing products that minimize environmental impact. Example: The Toyota Prius hybrid was one of the first mass-produced cars to offer reduced emissions and high fuel efficiency, appealing to environmentally conscious consumers.

9. **Conservation**: Incorporating features that conserve resources, such as energy or water. Example: Modern washing machines have settings that optimize water and energy use for different load sizes and soil levels.

10. **Customization**: Allowing customers to tailor the product to their specific preferences. Example: Nike By You (formerly NIKEiD) lets customers design their own sneakers with custom colors and materials.

11. **Focus**: Narrowing a product's functionality to serve a specific purpose or market niche very well. Example: GoPro cameras are focused on durability and portability for action and adventure photography.

12. **Styling**: Developing a distinctive aesthetic or design appeal of a product. Example: The sleek design of Beats by Dre headphones made them a status symbol as much as a piece of audio equipment.

Each of these tactics can be used to differentiate a product in the marketplace, meet specific customer needs, and add value to the product offering. They involve a deep understanding of customer preferences, market trends, and technological possibilities.

3.6 Product System

This dimension extends beyond individual products to consider complementary products and services. It's about creating a cohesive system, like building an ecosystem of products that work together or offering a suite of services that complement each other. Product system innovation tactics are about creating additional value around the core product through complementary services, features, or systems:

1. **Complements**: Products or services that add value to the primary product. Example: Apple's AirPods complement the iPhone, providing a seamless audio experience with the company's other devices.

2. **Extensions/Plug-ins**: Additional features or add-ons that can be attached to the main product to enhance its functionality. Example: Adobe Photoshop offers a vast array of plug-ins developed by Adobe and third-party companies, allowing users to greatly expand the software's capabilities.

3. **Product Bundling**: Offering several products or services together as a package deal. Example: Microsoft Office bundles together Word, Excel, PowerPoint, and other applications, providing a complete productivity suite.

4. **Modular Systems**: Designing products with interchangeable modules that can be replaced or upgraded as needed. Example: Lenovo's ThinkPad laptops have a modular design allowing users to swap out components like batteries and drives, thereby extending the laptop's longevity and customizability.

5. **Product/Service Platforms**: Establishing a base product or technology that other products or services are built upon. Example: Salesforce offers a customer relationship management platform that serves as a foundation for a suite of sales, marketing, and analytics services.

6. **Integrated Offering**: Combining products and services into a single, comprehensive solution. Example: Amazon Prime combines free shipping, streaming video, music services, and more, creating an integrated offering that enhances the value of the Amazon ecosystem.

By using these tactics, companies can not only improve customer satisfaction and loyalty but can also create barriers to competition, expand market share, and increase revenue through cross-selling and upselling opportunities.

3.7 Service

Innovating in service involves the ways in which you support, enhance, and amplify the value of your offerings. This could include customer support, maintenance services, or added-value services that improve the customer experience. Service innovation tactics involve creating value through new or improved ways of offering services to customers:

1. **Try Before You Buy**: Allowing customers to test a product or service before committing to a purchase. Example: Warby Parker offers a home try-on program where customers can select five frames to try at home for free, making the decision to purchase glasses easier and risk-free.

2. **Guarantee**: Providing a promise to customers to assure the quality of service. Example: Zappos offers a 365-day return policy with free

shipping both ways, guaranteeing customer satisfaction with their purchase.

3. **Loyalty Programs**: Rewarding regular customers to encourage repeat business. Example: Starbucks Rewards offers points for purchases that can be exchanged for free drinks and food, encouraging ongoing patronage.

4. **Added Value**: Providing additional services or benefits beyond the basic offering. Example: Many credit cards now offer travel insurance, concierge services, and extended warranties as added value to cardholders.

5. **Concierge**: Offering personalized services to handle various tasks or needs. Example: High-end hotels provide concierge services to assist guests with bookings, recommendations, and arranging special requests.

6. **Total Experience Management**: Ensuring that every aspect of the customer experience is managed to create satisfaction. Example: Disney theme parks meticulously design every aspect of the visit, from the attractions to the staff interactions, to ensure a magical experience.

7. **Supplementary Service**: Offering additional services that complement the primary service. Example: Car dealerships may offer maintenance services, loaner cars, and car washes as supplementary services to the primary service of selling vehicles.

8. **Superior Service**: Providing service that is superior to competitors in terms of speed, efficiency, or customer care. Example: Singapore Airlines is known for superior service, often ranking at the top for customer service in the airline industry.

9. **Personalized Service**: Tailoring the service to meet the specific needs or preferences of an individual customer. Example: Netflix provides personalized recommendations based on an individual's viewing history.

10. **User Communities/Support Systems**: Building platforms or forums where users can interact, solve problems, and share ideas. Example: Tech companies like Microsoft and Apple have support communities

where users can ask questions and receive help from both support staff and other users.

11. **Lease or Loan**: Offering products on a lease or loan basis, providing flexibility to customers. Example: Car manufacturers like BMW offer leasing options where customers can drive a car for a set period without the commitment of buying.

12. **Self-Service**: Enabling customers to serve themselves without the need for company intervention. Example: Self-checkout at supermarkets allows customers to scan and pay for their groceries without a cashier.

By deploying these service innovations, companies can enhance customer satisfaction, differentiate their service offerings, and potentially create new revenue streams.

3.8 Channel

This dimension relates to how a company delivers its products or services to customers. Innovating here could mean exploring new distribution channels, enhancing the customer journey, or using digital platforms to reach new markets. Channel innovation tactics focus on how companies deliver products and services to their customers through various distribution strategies:

1. **Diversification**: Using multiple channels to reach customers. Example: Nike uses a mix of its own retail stores, online sales, and partnerships with other retailers to sell its products.

2. **Flagship Store**: A company's main store, often in a prominent location, designed to be a showcase for the brand. Example: Apple's flagship stores are architectural marvels that provide an immersive brand experience.

3. **Go Direct**: Bypassing intermediaries and selling directly to consumers. Example: Dell was one of the first computer manufacturers to sell PCs directly to customers through its website, bypassing traditional retail channels.

4. **Non-traditional Channels**: Selling through channels that are unconventional for the product category. Example: Insurance

companies using supermarkets and retail stores to sell insurance policies.

5. **Pop-up Presence**: Temporary retail spaces that open for a short period of time to create a buzz. Example: Amazon has used pop-up shops in malls to promote its Echo devices during the holiday season.

6. **Indirect Distribution**: Selling through third-party intermediaries, such as distributors or wholesalers. Example: Procter & Gamble sells its products through various retailers rather than directly to consumers.

7. **Multi-Level Marketing (MLM)**: A strategy where sales representatives are compensated not only for sales they generate, but also for the sales of the other salespeople they recruit. Example: Beauty and wellness company Amway operates an MLM strategy.

8. **Cross-Selling**: Offering complementary products or services to an existing customer. Example: Banks often cross-sell insurance or investment products to their existing account holders.

9. **On-Demand**: Providing products or services as and when the customer needs them. Example: Uber offers rides on-demand, directly connecting drivers with passengers via its mobile app.

10. **Context Specific**: Tailoring the sales channel to fit the context in which the purchase decision is made. Example: Snack manufacturers place vending machines in airports, where travelers may need quick, on-the-go nourishment.

11. **Experience Center**: A showroom or space dedicated to giving customers a hands-on experience with products or services. Example: Samsung 837 in New York City is an experience center where customers can interact with Samsung's technology and products in innovative ways.

By innovating the channels through which they reach customers, companies can expand their market presence, create better customer experiences, and find new revenue opportunities.

3.9 BRANDING

Branding innovation involves how a company represents its offerings and business. This can include rebranding, brand extension, or developing a unique brand identity and narrative that resonates with customers and differentiates the company in the market. Branding innovation tactics involve strategies to enhance a brand's equity, reach, and customer perception:

1. **Co-Branding**: Partnering with another brand to take advantage of the synergy. Example: The partnership between Nike and Apple to create the Nike+ product line combines Nike's athletic expertise with Apple's technology prowess.

2. **Brand Leverage**: Utilizing the strength of an established brand to support a new product or venture. Example: Virgin Group leverages its brand across diverse sectors, from Virgin Atlantic (airlines) to Virgin Mobile (telecommunications).

3. **Private Label**: Retailers creating their own brand to sell exclusive products in their stores. Example: Target's "Up & Up" is a private label used for household items, offering a lower-cost alternative to national brands.

4. **Brand Extension**: Using an established brand name to launch products in a different category. Example: Porsche, known for sports cars, extended its brand into SUVs with the Porsche Cayenne.

5. **Component Branding**: Marketing a component of a product as a brand in its own right. Example: Intel's "Intel Inside" campaign made the microprocessor a key selling point for computers.

6. **Transparency**: Brands being open about their business practices, sourcing, and operations. Example: Patagonia's "Footprint Chronicles" provides consumers with transparency about the environmental impact of its products.

7. **Values Alignment**: Ensuring that brand values align with customer values to create a strong brand connection. Example: Ben & Jerry's aligns its brand with social justice causes, resonating with consumers who share similar values.

8. **Certification**: Gaining third-party certification to reinforce the brand's claims about product quality or sustainability. Example: Fair Trade certification on coffee brands indicates support for better trading conditions and sustainable farming.

These tactics can help brands differentiate themselves, create deeper customer loyalty, and expand their market presence.

3.10 CUSTOMER ENGAGEMENT

This is about the interactions between the company and its customers. Innovating in customer engagement might involve personalized communication, building online communities, creating memorable experiences, or using customer feedback to shape offerings. Engagement innovation tactics are designed to enhance how customers interact with a brand or product, focusing on creating a more compelling, personalized, and enjoyable experience:

1. **Process Automation**: Simplifying customer interactions by automating routine processes. Example: Chatbots on websites provide instant customer service, automating the resolution of common queries.

2. **Experience Simplification**: Making it easier for customers to navigate and use products or services. Example: Amazon's 1-Click ordering simplifies the online purchasing process.

3. **Curation**: Selecting and presenting a range of products or content tailored to individual tastes. Example: Spotify curates personalized playlists based on listeners' streaming history.

4. **Experience Enabling**: Providing tools or resources that enable customers to have a better experience with the product. Example: IKEA's augmented reality app allows customers to visualize how furniture would look in their homes.

5. **Mastery**: Allowing customers to develop a deeper understanding or skill in relation to a product. Example: Adobe Creative Cloud includes tutorials and templates that help users master its software.

6. **Autonomy and Authority**: Giving customers the freedom to customize or have control over their experience. Example: The video game "Minecraft" gives players the autonomy to build and explore virtual worlds without a set of defined goals.

7. **Community and Belonging**: Creating a sense of community among customers, where they feel a sense of belonging and shared purpose.

Example: Harley-Davidson fosters a strong brand community with clubs and events for motorcycle enthusiasts.

8. **Personalization**: Tailoring the customer experience to individual needs or preferences. Example: Netflix's algorithm personalizes viewing recommendations for each user.

9. **Whimsy and Personality**: Incorporating fun, personality, and unexpected elements into the customer experience. Example: MailChimp's friendly and humorous tone in its communications and error messages adds whimsy to its email marketing service.

10. **Status and Recognition**: Providing recognition to customers that enhances their status. Example: Frequent flyer programs offer status levels that come with perks, recognition, and a sense of prestige among travelers.

These tactics help create a deeper emotional connection with customers, increase customer satisfaction, and encourage brand loyalty.

Each dimension offers a distinct avenue for innovation, allowing companies to explore various aspects of their business model and operational approach. By considering these dimensions, businesses can identify new opportunities for growth and competitive advantage.

4 Clayton Christensen's Typology of Innovations

Clayton Christensen was a renowned scholar and professor at Harvard Business School, widely recognized for his groundbreaking work in the field of innovation and business management. His most influential work, "The Innovator's Dilemma," published in 1997, introduced concepts that have become foundational in understanding how businesses grow, evolve, and respond to technological changes and market forces. Christensen's insights have not only shaped academic discourse but have also profoundly influenced the strategies of numerous organizations worldwide.

A New Framework for Understanding Innovation: Christensen's work is particularly notable for its categorization of innovation into three distinct types: Disruptive Innovation, Sustaining Innovation, and Efficiency Innovation. This framework offers a nuanced understanding of how innovation impacts industries and markets, and how businesses can adapt and thrive in a rapidly changing landscape.

4.1 Disruptive Innovation

4.1.1 Defining Disruptive Innovation:

Disruptive innovation, a term coined by Clayton Christensen, refers to a process where a smaller company with fewer resources successfully challenges established incumbent businesses. Unlike innovations that make incremental improvements to existing products or services, disruptive innovations redefine markets, often by introducing simplicity, convenience, accessibility, and affordability where complexity and high cost are the status quo.

4.1.2 Characteristics of Disruptive Innovation:

- **Emergence in Niche Markets**: Disruptive innovations often gain a foothold in small, niche markets. Initially, they may appear less attractive or inferior to mainstream offerings, targeting customers whose needs are ignored by the larger players.
- **Gradual Market Domination**: Over time, these innovations improve, achieving a quality acceptable to a broader range of customers and start

to capture a significant share of the market, eventually displacing established competitors.

- **Cost-effectiveness**: Often, disruptive products or services are more affordable than existing alternatives, making them accessible to a larger portion of the population.

4.1.3 Examples of Disruptive Innovation:

- **Digital Photography vs. Film Photography**: Digital photography, with its convenience and lower cost of operation, gradually displaced film photography. It democratized photography, making it accessible to millions who could not afford the ongoing costs of film.

- **Cloud-based Solutions vs. Traditional On-premise Software**: Cloud computing disrupted traditional IT industries by offering scalable, pay-as-you-go services. Businesses no longer needed to invest heavily in on-premise infrastructure, leading to a significant shift in how IT services are consumed and paid for.

4.1.4 Challenges and Strategic Responses:

- **Identifying Disruptive Opportunities**: Companies must learn to recognize the early signs of potential disruption in their industries. This involves understanding customer needs, especially those that are currently underserved, and monitoring emerging technologies.

- **Responding to Disruption**: Established companies facing disruption need to be agile and willing to adapt their business models. This may involve setting up independent units focused on the disruptive innovation, separate from the core business.

- **Balancing Core and New Businesses**: For incumbents, one of the biggest challenges is balancing resources and attention between the existing core business and the potentially disruptive new business.

Disruptive innovation represents both a threat and an opportunity. While it poses significant challenges to incumbent firms, it also offers opportunities for startups and existing companies willing to explore new market niches and experiment with new business models. Successfully navigating disruptive innovation requires a keen understanding of market dynamics, customer needs, and the ability to rapidly adapt and innovate.

4.2 Sustaining Innovation

4.2.1 Defining Sustaining Innovation:
Sustaining innovations are typically the kind of improvements we see in most industries; they make products better, faster, or more efficient, but they do not fundamentally change the market's landscape. These innovations are crucial for companies to stay competitive and to keep their products relevant and appealing to their existing customer base.

4.2.2 Characteristics of Sustaining Innovation:
- **Targeting Existing Markets and Customers:** Unlike disruptive innovations, sustaining innovations focus on the same customer base with the goal of offering them a better version of what they already use.

- **Evolutionary, Not Revolutionary:** These innovations are usually more about refinement than reinvention, providing incremental changes that improve performance or reduce costs.

- **Compatibility with Current Business Models**: Sustaining innovations typically fit well within a company's existing business model and often strengthen the company's position in its current markets.

4.2.3 Examples of Sustaining Innovation:
- **Smartphones**: The evolution of smartphones is a prime example of sustaining innovation. Each new model offers improvements like better cameras, faster processors, and longer battery life, but the basic market and user experience remain unchanged.

- **Medical Equipment**: Continuous advancements in medical technology, such as more precise imaging equipment or more effective surgical tools, provide better diagnostics and treatment options without altering the fundamental healthcare delivery system.

4.2.4 Management Considerations for Sustaining Innovation:
- **Consistent Focus on Improvement**: Companies need to establish a culture that continually seeks to improve existing products and services. This involves regular investment in R&D and staying attuned to the evolving needs of their customer base.

- **Balancing Innovation and Core Products**: It's crucial to strike a balance between innovating and maintaining the quality and profitability of current products. Companies must manage their resources to ensure that sustaining innovations do not cannibalize or detract from their existing offerings.
- **Integrating Innovations**: Successfully implementing sustaining innovations often requires careful planning to integrate these improvements into existing production, marketing, and distribution channels.

Sustaining innovation is essential for the ongoing success and competitiveness of any business. It allows companies to grow and evolve within their existing markets and to keep their offerings aligned with the needs and expectations of their customers. While it may not capture headlines like disruptive innovations, sustaining innovation is the backbone of long-term business growth and stability.

4.3 Efficiency Innovation

4.3.1 Defining Efficiency Innovation:

Efficiency innovations are aimed at reducing the cost of production and distribution of goods and services. They are crucial for improving the profitability of businesses and often involve optimizing various aspects of the operational process. While these innovations might not lead to new products or services, they play a significant role in enhancing the efficiency and competitiveness of companies.

4.3.2 Characteristics of Efficiency Innovation:
- **Cost Reduction and Efficiency**: The primary goal of efficiency innovation is to decrease operational costs and increase process efficiency, often achieved through technological advancements, process redesign, or optimization.
- **Resource Optimization**: These innovations often involve doing more with less—utilizing fewer resources, less time, or less labor to produce the same or improved outcomes.

- **Incorporation of New Technologies**: Frequently, efficiency innovation involves the adoption of new technologies such as automation, digital tools, and advanced machinery.

4.3.3 Examples of Efficiency Innovation:
- **Robotics in Manufacturing**: Many manufacturing industries have integrated robotics into their production lines. Robots increase production efficiency, accuracy, and safety while reducing labor costs and human error.
- **Self-Service Checkouts in Retail**: Supermarkets and retail stores have implemented self-service checkouts, which reduce the need for a large number of cashiers and expedite the checkout process for customers.

4.3.4 Implications of Efficiency Innovation:
- **Economic Impact**: While efficiency innovations can significantly boost profitability and market competitiveness, they can also lead to job reductions in certain sectors as processes become more automated.
- **Workforce Reskilling**: There is an increasing need for workforce reskilling and retraining to prepare employees for a changing job landscape where many traditional roles are automated.
- **Short-term vs. Long-term Impacts**: In the short term, efficiency innovations can lead to cost savings for companies and lower prices for consumers. However, in the long term, they can contribute to significant shifts in labor markets and economic structures.

Efficiency innovation plays a vital role in the modern business landscape, allowing companies to stay competitive in a global market by reducing costs and improving operational efficiencies. However, the drive for efficiency must be balanced with considerations for its broader economic and social implications, particularly concerning employment and workforce development. As businesses continue to innovate for greater efficiency, they also face the challenge of ensuring that their workforce evolves alongside these changes.

4.4 COMPARATIVE ANALYSIS: IMPACT ON BUSINESS STRATEGY AND GROWTH
- **Disruptive Innovation**: While potentially risky, disruptive innovation can open entirely new markets and opportunities, offering substantial long-

term growth potential. However, it requires a willingness to venture into uncharted territory and possibly cannibalize existing products.

- **Sustaining Innovation**: Essential for keeping existing products and services competitive, sustaining innovation helps firms to maintain market relevance and customer satisfaction. It's critical for steady, incremental growth and defending market position.

- **Efficiency Innovation**: Improves profit margins and operational efficiency but may not drive substantial growth. It's vital for maintaining profitability and freeing up resources that can be invested in other types of innovation.

4.5 Integration for Success: Blending Different Innovation Types

- **Balanced Approach**: Companies should strive for a balanced portfolio of all three types of innovation. While disruptive innovations explore new frontiers, sustaining and efficiency innovations optimize and protect the core business.

- **Resource Allocation**: Allocate resources strategically across different types of innovation, understanding that each serves different but complementary roles in the business.

- **Culture and Leadership**: Foster a culture of innovation that encourages experimentation and is tolerant of failure, especially in pursuing disruptive and sustaining innovations. Leadership should actively support and champion innovation initiatives.

4.6 Future Outlook: The Evolving Nature of Innovation

- **Continual Evolution**: The landscape of innovation is continuously evolving with advancements in technology and changes in consumer behavior. Companies need to be agile and forward-thinking to adapt to these changes.

- **Embracing Change and Uncertainty**: The future will likely hold new forms of disruptive innovation that we can't currently predict. Organizations must be prepared to embrace change and navigate uncertainty.

- **Sustainable and Social Innovation**: There is an increasing trend towards innovations that are not only economically viable but also socially responsible and sustainable. Companies will need to consider the broader impact of their innovations on society and the environment.

References for Further Reading:

1. Christensen, Clayton M. "The Innovator's Dilemma: When New Technologies Cause Great Firms to Fail." Harvard Business Review Press.
2. Christensen, Clayton M., et al. "The Innovator's Solution: Creating and Sustaining Successful Growth." Harvard Business Review Press.
3. Christensen, Clayton M., et al. "Seeing What's Next: Using Theories of Innovation to Predict Industry Change." Harvard Business Review Press.
4. Anthony, Scott D. "The Little Black Book of Innovation: How It Works, How to Do It." Harvard Business Review Press.
5. Christensen, Clayton M. "How Will You Measure Your Life?" Harper Business.
6. Dyer, Jeff, et al. "The Innovator's DNA: Mastering the Five Skills of Disruptive Innovators." Harvard Business Review Press.

5 MODELS OF INNOVATION

5.1 TECHNOLOGY PUSH MODEL OF INNOVATION (1950s)

The Technology Push Model of innovation, developed in the 1950s, represents one of the earliest conceptual frameworks for understanding the innovation process. This model suggests that the primary impetus for innovation begins with technological advancements made by researchers and developers, which are then pushed into the market.

5.1.1 Core Concept of the Technology Push Model:
- **Sequential Process**: The model proposes a linear progression of innovation, starting from scientific research and development (R&D) and moving towards manufacturing, marketing, and eventually reaching the consumers.
- **Origin of Innovation**: Innovations are seen as being driven by technological breakthroughs and discoveries, often in isolation from market demand.
- **Role of R&D**: Research and development are viewed as the starting point and the driving force of the innovation process. The emphasis is on the capabilities and activities within research labs or technical departments.

5.1.2 Dynamics of the Technology Push Model:
- **Innovation Initiation**: Innovations begin as scientific and technical ideas or discoveries.
- **Development and Production**: These ideas are developed into tangible products or processes, followed by production.
- **Market Introduction**: The final stage involves introducing the new product or process into the market, often accompanied by efforts to create demand among consumers.

5.1.3 Examples and Applications:
- **Pharmaceutical Industry**: Many drugs begin as scientific discoveries in laboratories, followed by clinical trials and, if successful, eventual introduction to the healthcare market.

- **Space Technology**: Innovations in space technology, such as satellite communication, originated from scientific research and were later commercialized.

5.1.4 Critique and Limitations:
- **Market Neglect**: One criticism of the Technology Push Model is its lack of consideration for market needs or consumer feedback during the early stages of the innovation process.
- **Linear Perspective**: The model's linear perspective on innovation has been considered overly simplistic, not accounting for the more complex, iterative, and interactive nature of modern innovation processes.

While the Technology Push Model provides a foundational understanding of how technological advancements can initiate the innovation process, it is important to recognize its limitations. Modern innovation models tend to emphasize a more integrated approach, considering both technological capabilities and market needs. Nonetheless, the Technology Push Model remains an important part of the history of innovation theory, underlining the significance of R&D in the innovation ecosystem.

5.2 MARKET PULL MODEL OF INNOVATION (1960s)

Emerging in the 1960s as a counterpoint to the Technology Push Model, the Market Pull Model of innovation posits that the primary driver of innovation is market demand. This model suggests that the innovation process starts with a market opportunity, where customers' needs and wants create a demand that pulls technologies through development and into the market.

5.2.1 Fundamentals of the Market Pull Model:
- **Demand-Driven Innovation**: Unlike the Technology Push Model, where innovation is driven by technological capabilities, the Market Pull Model asserts that customer needs and market demands are the main catalysts for innovation.
- **Identification of Market Needs**: The process begins with identifying a need or problem in the market, often through market research or customer feedback.

- **Development Aligned with Market Demand**: Innovations are then developed specifically to address these identified market needs, ensuring that the end product meets consumer expectations.

5.2.2 The Process of Market Pull Innovation:

1. **Market Need Identification**: Recognizing a gap or an unmet need in the market through consumer insights or market analysis.
2. **R&D and Product Development**: Developing products or services that specifically address the identified needs.
3. **Market Introduction**: Introducing the innovation to the market, where it has been anticipated and is pulled in by consumer demand.

5.2.3 Examples of Market Pull Innovations:

- **Consumer Electronics**: Many features in smartphones, such as improved cameras and battery life, are developed in response to consumer demand and feedback.
- **Eco-Friendly Products**: The increasing demand for sustainable and eco-friendly products has led companies to innovate and offer green alternatives in various industries.

5.2.4 Advantages and Critiques:

- **Alignment with Consumer Needs**: A key advantage of the Market Pull Model is that it ensures innovations are closely aligned with consumer needs, potentially leading to higher acceptance and success in the market.
- **Reactive Nature**: A critique of this model is that it can be overly reactive, focusing on current needs without anticipating future trends or technological possibilities.

The Market Pull Model highlights the importance of understanding and responding to market demands in the innovation process. It underscores the necessity for businesses to remain customer-focused and responsive to market trends. However, the most effective innovation strategies often integrate both market pull and technology push elements, balancing market needs with technological possibilities.

5.3 The Coupling Model of Innovation (Rothwell, 1994)

Proposed by Roy Rothwell in 1994, the Coupling Model of innovation emerged as a response to the limitations of the linear models of innovation (Technology Push and Market Pull). The Coupling Model advocates for a more integrated and interactive approach to innovation, emphasizing the interplay between technology push, market pull, and other factors.

5.3.1 Key Features of the Coupling Model:

- **Interactive Process**: This model views innovation as an interactive process where feedback loops between different stages and actors (including R&D, manufacturing, marketing, and sales) are essential.

- **Integration of Market and Technology**: Unlike the linear models, the Coupling Model suggests that successful innovation requires a balance and coupling of both market needs and technological capabilities.

- **Multiple Influences**: It acknowledges that innovation is influenced by a range of factors, including government policies, firm strategy, the competitive environment, and societal changes.

5.3.2 The Process of Coupled Innovation:

1. **Idea Generation**: Involving both technological possibilities and market needs.

2. **Development**: Interaction and feedback between design, production, and market research teams are crucial.

3. **Commercialization**: Launching the product involves continued adjustments based on market feedback and technological advancements.

4. **Continuous Improvement**: Post-launch, the innovation is refined and improved through ongoing customer feedback and technological development.

5.3.3 Applications of the Coupling Model:

- **Technology and Consumer Electronics**: Firms in these sectors often have to rapidly adapt to both technological advancements and evolving consumer preferences.

- **Pharmaceuticals and Biotechnology**: Innovation in these industries typically requires a close coupling of scientific research (technology push) with patient needs and regulatory requirements (market pull).

5.3.4 Advantages of the Coupling Model:
- **Comprehensive Approach**: By considering multiple factors and feedback loops, the model offers a more realistic and holistic approach to innovation.
- **Adaptability**: The interactive nature of the model allows firms to be more adaptable and responsive to changes in technology and the market.

The Coupling Model represents an evolution in the understanding of innovation processes, highlighting the importance of interaction and integration of various elements. It provides a framework for organizations to strategically approach innovation, considering both internal capabilities and external market dynamics. In today's fast-paced and interconnected world, this model is particularly relevant for businesses aiming to navigate the complexities of innovation effectively.

5.4 FOUR DIMENSION OF INNOVATION SPACE

The 4 Ps Innovation model, developed by Professors John Bessant and Joe Tidd, presents a comprehensive framework for understanding and implementing innovation. It extends beyond the traditional focus on products to encompass all aspects that can be innovated within a business: Product, Process, Position, and Paradigm.

5.4.1 Product Innovation
Product innovation is the most visible form of innovation. It involves the development of new products or significant improvements to existing ones. This type of innovation is directly experienced by customers and can range from introducing cutting-edge technology to making incremental improvements in current offerings.

- **Example**: Apple Inc.'s development of the iPhone revolutionized the mobile phone industry, combining a phone, an internet device, and a music player into one product.

5.4.2 Process Innovation

Process innovation focuses on improving or creating new methods for production, delivery, and support. It aims to enhance efficiency, quality, and customer service. Though less visible to consumers, process innovation can significantly impact an organization's effectiveness and bottom line.

- **Example**: Toyota's implementation of the Just-In-Time (JIT) production system significantly reduced inventory costs and improved manufacturing efficiency.

5.4.3 Position Innovation

Position innovation involves changing the context or perception of a product or service. It doesn't necessarily involve changing the product itself but rather how it is positioned in the market. This can include targeting new market segments, rebranding, or altering the marketing strategy.

- **Example**: Starbucks' repositioning from selling coffee beans and equipment to offering a complete coffee experience transformed the perception of coffee shops.

5.4.4 Paradigm Innovation

Paradigm innovation is the most profound level of innovation. It involves changing the underlying mental models and assumptions on which a business operates. This type of innovation can redefine the industry norms and lead to significant shifts in market dynamics.

- **Example**: Netflix's shift from DVD rentals to streaming services changed the paradigm in the entertainment distribution industry.

5.4.5 Interplay of Incremental and Radical Innovation

The 4 Ps model also illustrates how incremental and radical innovations can coexist within these categories. Incremental innovations are small yet impactful improvements, while radical innovations represent significant shifts, opening up new markets or redefining existing ones.

5.4.6 Applying the 4 Ps of Innovation in Business

- Companies can use this model to systematically explore different areas for innovation.

- Encourages a holistic view of innovation, ensuring that all aspects of the business are considered for potential improvements.

The 4 Ps of Innovation model provides a multidimensional framework for businesses to navigate the complex terrain of innovation. By embracing this model, companies can go beyond product development to innovate in processes, positioning, and paradigms, ensuring comprehensive growth and sustainability in the market.

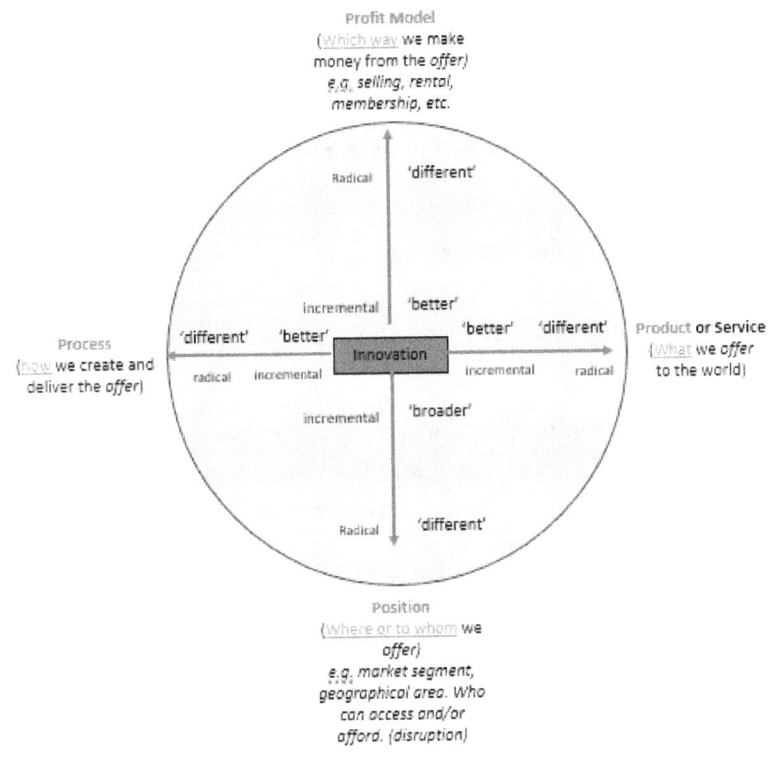

5.5 OPEN INNOVATION MODEL (CHESBROUGH, 2003)

Introduced by Henry Chesbrough in 2003, the Open Innovation Model marked a paradigm shift in how companies approach innovation. It challenges the traditional view of innovation being confined within the walls of a company, advocating instead for leveraging external as well as internal ideas and paths to market.

5.5.1 Key Concepts of the Open Innovation Model:

- **Definition**: Open Innovation is the practice of businesses' actively using external ideas and innovations in conjunction with their internal research and development.

- **Inbound Open Innovation**: Involves bringing in ideas, insights, and technologies from outside the organization to drive internal innovation.

- **Outbound Open Innovation**: Refers to the external exploitation of internal ideas or technologies, for example, through licensing, joint ventures, or spin-offs.

5.5.2 The Shift from Closed to Open Innovation:

- **Closed Innovation Model**: Traditionally, companies relied on their internal R&D for all their innovations and kept their intellectual property tightly secured.

- **Evolution to Open Innovation**: Increasingly, companies recognize that not all the smartest people work for them and that they can benefit from a broader innovation ecosystem that includes academia, startups, competitors, and even customers.

5.5.3 Applications and Examples:

- **Collaborative Research and Development**: Companies collaborating with universities or research institutes for cutting-edge research.

- **Crowdsourcing**: Leveraging the collective knowledge and skills of a large group of people, often through online platforms, to solve problems or generate ideas.

- **Corporate Venture Capital**: Investing in external startups to gain insight into new technologies and business models.

5.5.4 Benefits and Challenges:

- **Advantages**: Access to a wider pool of ideas, reduction in R&D costs, acceleration of innovation processes, and potential for creating new revenue streams.

- **Challenges**: Includes managing intellectual property rights, cultural barriers within organizations, and integrating external knowledge with internal processes.

The Open Innovation Model represents a more dynamic, collaborative, and outward-looking approach to innovation. It acknowledges that in a world of widely distributed knowledge, companies cannot afford to rely solely on their internal resources but should instead capitalize on the wealth of ideas outside their boundaries. This model has significant implications for how companies strategize, collaborate, and compete in the current era of rapid technological advancement and globalization.

5.6 TEN TYPES OF INNOVATION (DOBLIN, 1990S)

In the 1990s, the innovation firm Doblin, founded by Larry Keeley, identified Ten Types of Innovation, a framework that broadened the perspective on innovation beyond just product or technology. This framework categorizes innovation into three main areas: Configuration, Offering, and Experience, each containing specific types of innovation.

5.6.1 The Ten Types of Innovation:

1. **Profit Model**: How a company makes money. Innovating in the profit model involves finding new ways to generate revenue and profit.

2. **Network**: How a company connects with others to create value. Innovations in network involve partnerships, collaborations, and distribution channels.

3. **Structure**: How a company organizes and aligns its talent and assets. Structural innovations can include new teams, departments, or business units.

4. **Process**: How a company uses unique methods to do its work. Process innovation can be about streamlining operations, improving production, or implementing new technologies.

5. **Product Performance**: Enhancements and innovations in a company's core offerings. This can include new features, functionalities, or design improvements.

6. **Product System**: How a company creates complementary products and services. This can involve systems of products that work together or ecosystem strategies.

7. **Service**: How a company supports and amplifies the value of its offerings. Innovations in service can improve customer support, maintenance, or additional service offerings.

8. **Channel**: How a company delivers its offerings to customers and users. Channel innovations can involve new sales channels, distribution methods, or delivery mechanisms.

9. **Brand**: How a company represents its offerings and business. Brand innovations can include new branding strategies, marketing campaigns, or public relations efforts.

10. **Customer Engagement**: How a company fosters distinctive interactions. Innovations in customer engagement involve improving the customer experience, personalized communications, or community building.

5.6.2 Applications and Implications:

- **Holistic Approach to Innovation**: The framework suggests that companies should look beyond product innovation and explore other areas where they can innovate.

- **Strategic Planning**: It serves as a tool for organizations to audit their current innovation strategies and identify new areas for growth.

- **Competitive Advantage**: By innovating across multiple areas, companies can create a more robust and sustainable competitive advantage.

5.6.3 Examples of Application:

- **Apple Inc.**: Apple's innovation goes beyond products (like the iPhone) to include its profit model (iTunes music sales), service (AppleCare), and customer engagement (Apple Stores and community).

- **Airbnb**: Airbnb innovated in its profit model (sharing economy), network (connecting hosts with guests), and customer engagement (user-friendly platform and community-driven experiences).

The Ten Types of Innovation framework provides a comprehensive lens through which businesses can assess and enhance their innovation strategies. By exploring these different types, companies can uncover new opportunities for growth and differentiation in an increasingly competitive market.

5.7 LEAN STARTUP METHODOLOGY (ERIC RIES, 2008)

Developed by Eric Ries in 2008, the Lean Startup Methodology is a business approach that advocates for a more efficient, iterative model of developing products and businesses. This methodology is particularly influential in the world of startups and entrepreneurship, offering a systematic, scientific approach for creating and managing successful startups in an age of uncertainty and rapid innovation.

5.7.1 Core Principles of Lean Startup:

1. **Build-Measure-Learn Loop**: The central tenet of Lean Startup is the Build-Measure-Learn feedback loop. Startups should quickly build a Minimum Viable Product (MVP), measure its effectiveness in the market, and learn from the experience to make necessary adjustments.

2. **Validated Learning**: Instead of traditional business planning, Lean Startup emphasizes validated learning, a process of quickly testing ideas and hypotheses about the business model and customer needs.

3. **Pivot or Persevere**: Based on feedback and learning, startups decide whether to pivot (make a fundamental change to the product or strategy) or persevere (continue with the current path).

5.7.2 Implementation of Lean Startup:

- **Minimum Viable Product (MVP)**: Creating and launching a product with just enough features to satisfy early customers and provide feedback for future development.

- **Customer Development**: Actively engaging with customers to validate assumptions about the market and understand their needs and preferences.

- **Agile Development**: Borrowing from agile software development, this involves short development cycles focused on continuous improvement and flexibility to change.

5.7.3 Benefits and Challenges:
- **Efficiency and Speed**: Lean Startup helps to reduce both time and resources wasted on developing products that customers don't want.
- **Risk Mitigation**: By testing the market early and frequently, the methodology helps reduce the risks inherent in startup ventures.
- **Adaptability**: Encourages startups to be adaptable, learning from failures and adapting their strategies quickly.
- **Challenges**: Implementing this methodology requires a cultural shift in many organizations, emphasizing flexibility, continuous learning, and a high tolerance for failure.

5.7.4 Applications and Examples:
- **Tech Startups**: Many tech startups use Lean Startup principles to quickly launch new software products, gather user feedback, and iterate on their designs.
- **Corporate Innovation**: Large companies are increasingly adopting Lean Startup techniques to drive innovation within their organizations, applying the principles to new product development and internal processes.

The Lean Startup Methodology provides a blueprint for managing startups and new ventures in a methodical way, emphasizing experimentation, customer feedback, and iterative design. Its impact goes beyond startups, influencing how companies of all sizes and industries approach product development and innovation in an uncertain business environment.

5.8 Gartner Hype Cycle in Innovation

The Gartner Hype Cycle is a graphical representation of the maturity, adoption, and social application of specific technologies. Developed by Gartner, a global research and advisory firm, this tool provides a snapshot of the relative market promotion and perception of technologies. It's a valuable instrument for organizations to understand the evolving landscape of technology-driven innovation.

5.8.1 Structure of the Gartner Hype Cycle

The Hype Cycle is characterized by five key phases:

1. **Technology Trigger**: The technology is conceptualized, leading to significant interest and publicity.
2. **Peak of Inflated Expectations**: Early publicity generates over-enthusiasm and unrealistic expectations.
3. **Trough of Disillusionment**: Interest wanes as experiments and implementations fail to deliver.
4. **Slope of Enlightenment**: More instances of how the technology can benefit the enterprise start to crystallize.
5. **Plateau of Productivity**: Mainstream adoption starts to take off; the technology's practical benefits are demonstrated and accepted.

5.8.2 Application in Innovation Management

- **Strategic Planning**: Assisting businesses in making informed decisions about which technologies to invest in.
- **Market Analysis**: Understanding the evolving trends and potential of emerging technologies.
- **Risk Management**: Identifying and managing the risks associated with investing in new technologies.

5.8.3 Benefits of the Gartner Hype Cycle

- **Insights into Technology Trends**: Provides a snapshot of how technologies are evolving.
- **Decision-Making Support**: Offers a framework to assess the maturity and potential impact of technologies.
- **Innovation Strategy Development**: Aids in developing strategies aligned with the maturity stages of various technologies.

5.8.4 Examples of Technologies on the Gartner Hype Cycle

1. **Virtual Reality (VR)**: Initially at the Peak of Inflated Expectations with much hype, VR moved through the Trough of Disillusionment as challenges in implementation were encountered, and is now advancing towards the Plateau of Productivity as practical applications are developed.

2. **Blockchain**: Blockchain technology experienced rapid movement through the early stages of the Hype Cycle and is currently navigating the Trough of Disillusionment as practical and sustainable use cases are being developed beyond cryptocurrency.

5.8.5 Challenges in Using the Gartner Hype Cycle

- **Dynamic Nature of Technology**: The rapid evolution of technology can make the Hype Cycle a moving target.
- **Subjectivity**: The positioning of technologies can be somewhat subjective and open to interpretation.
- **Over-reliance**: Relying solely on the Hype Cycle for investment decisions without considering specific organizational contexts.

5.8.6 Best Practices for Leveraging the Gartner Hype Cycle

- **Complementary Analysis**: Use the Hype Cycle in conjunction with other analytical tools and market research.
- **Contextual Application**: Apply insights from the Hype Cycle in the context of your organization's specific needs and capabilities.
- **Continuous Monitoring**: Keep abreast of changes in the Hype Cycle as technology markets are fast-evolving.

The Gartner Hype Cycle offers a strategic lens for viewing the progression of technology innovations, helping businesses to navigate the complexities of new technologies. By understanding where a technology lies on the Hype Cycle, organizations can make more informed decisions about technology adoption and investment.

5.9 Technology Readiness Levels in Innovation

Technology Readiness Levels (TRLs) are a method of estimating the maturity of technologies during the acquisition phase of a program. Developed initially by NASA, TRLs are now widely used in industry and government to assess the maturity of a technology from the concept stage to its full deployment.

5.9.1 Understanding Technology Readiness Levels

TRLs are divided into nine levels:

Research

1. **Basic principles observed and reported** - Earliest stage of technology discovery.
2. **Technology concept and/or application formulated** - Conceptualization stage.
3. **Analytical and experimental critical function and/or characteristic proof of concept** - Initial proof of concept developed.

Development

4. **Component and/or breadboard validation in laboratory environment** - Technology tested in lab.
5. **Component and/or breadboard validation in relevant environment** - Initial validation in relevant environment.
6. **System/subsystem model or prototype demonstration in a relevant environment** - Prototype demonstration.

Deployment

7. **System prototype demonstration in an operational environment** - Advanced prototype testing.
8. **Actual system completed and qualified through test and demonstration** - System completed and tested in operational scenarios.
9. **Actual system proven through successful mission operations** - Proven system deployment and operation.

5.9.2 Application of TRLs in Innovation

- **Research and Development Planning**: Guiding R&D activities from basic research to product development.
- **Funding and Investment Decisions**: Assessing technology maturity for funding and investment decisions.
- **Risk Management**: Identifying technological risks at different stages of development.

5.9.3 Benefits of Using TRLs

- **Standardized Assessment**: Provides a standardized framework for assessing technology maturity.
- **Informed Decision-Making**: Aids in making informed decisions regarding technology development and investments.
- **Communication Tool**: Facilitates clear communication about technology status among different stakeholders.

5.9.4 Examples of Technology Readiness Levels in Practice

1. **Space Exploration Technologies**: NASA uses TRLs to assess the readiness of new technologies for space missions, such as propulsion systems or life support systems.
2. **Clean Energy Technologies**: Renewable energy companies might use TRLs to evaluate the development stages of new solar panel or wind turbine technologies.

5.9.5 Challenges in Implementing TRLs

- **Subjective Assessment**: Determining the specific TRL can be subjective and dependent on the assessor's judgment.
- **Applicability to Different Technologies**: Adapting the TRL framework to different types of technologies across various industries.
- **Integration with Business Processes**: Aligning TRL assessments with business and innovation processes.

5.9.6 Best Practices for Applying TRLs

- **Clear Definition and Training**: Ensure that all team members understand the TRL definitions and criteria.

- **Regular Reviews and Updates**: Regularly review and update the TRL assessment as the technology develops.
- **Complementary Tools**: Use TRLs in conjunction with other project management and risk assessment tools.

Technology Readiness Levels provide a valuable framework for assessing the maturity and viability of new technologies in the innovation process. By effectively applying TRLs, organizations can better manage the development of technologies, making informed decisions and reducing risks associated with technological innovation.

5.10 THE GOLDEN CIRCLE IN INNOVATION

The Golden Circle is a concept developed by Simon Sinek, focusing on why, how, and what as key elements of successful communication and leadership. In the realm of innovation, the Golden Circle framework can be a powerful tool to understand and articulate the purpose, process, and product of innovation initiatives.

5.10.1 Understanding the Golden Circle
- **Why**: This is the core belief, the purpose, or the reason why the company exists.
- **How**: These are the specific actions or processes taken to realize the 'Why'.
- **What**: This refers to the end product or the result of the 'Why' and 'How'.

5.10.2 Application in Innovation Management
- **Inspiring Innovation**: Starting with 'Why' can inspire and motivate teams, aligning them with the deeper purpose behind the innovation.
- **Guiding Product Development**: Clarifying 'How' can streamline the development process, ensuring that every action aligns with the core purpose.

- **Marketing and Communication**: The 'What' becomes more compelling when grounded in a strong 'Why' and 'How', enhancing market acceptance and success.

5.10.3 Benefits of Using the Golden Circle in Innovation
- **Clearer Vision**: Provides a clear understanding of the purpose behind innovation efforts.
- **Aligned Strategies**: Ensures that strategies and actions are in alignment with the core purpose.
- **Enhanced Team Engagement**: Motivates and engages teams by connecting them to a meaningful purpose.

5.10.4 Examples of the Golden Circle in Innovation
1. **Apple Inc.**: Apple starts with 'Why' - challenging the status quo and thinking differently. Their 'How' is by creating beautifully designed, user-friendly products, leading to 'What' - their range of innovative products like iPhones and MacBooks.
2. **Tesla, Inc.**: Tesla's 'Why' is to accelerate the world's transition to sustainable energy. Their 'How' involves developing cutting-edge electric vehicles and renewable energy solutions, resulting in products like the Model S and solar panels.

5.10.5 Challenges in Implementing the Golden Circle
- **Identifying the True 'Why'**: It can be challenging to delve deep and articulate a genuine and compelling 'Why'.
- **Consistency Across Levels**: Ensuring that the 'How' and 'What' consistently align with the 'Why' at all levels of the innovation process.
- **Over-Simplification**: Avoiding the oversimplification of complex innovation processes.

5.10.6 Best Practices for the Golden Circle in Innovation
- **Deep Exploration**: Spend significant time uncovering and articulating the 'Why'.
- **Consistent Messaging**: Ensure that all communications and actions are consistent with the defined 'Why', 'How', and 'What'.

- **Employee Involvement**: Involve employees at all levels in understanding and embracing the Golden Circle framework.

The Golden Circle framework offers a structured approach to thinking about and communicating innovation. By starting with 'Why', innovators can create more meaningful, impactful, and successful innovations that resonate with both their teams and their target markets.

5.11 Business Model Canvas (Osterwalder and Pigneur, 2010)

Business Model Canvas, developed by Alexander Osterwalder and Yves Pigneur in their 2010 book "Business Model Generation," presents a visual chart with elements describing a company's or product's value proposition, infrastructure, customers, and finances. It offers an alternative to traditional business plans by providing a more flexible and concise way to conceptualize and communicate business models.

5.11.1 Key Components of the Business Model Canvas:

The canvas is divided into nine building blocks:

1. **Customer Segments**: Defines the different groups of people or organizations the business aims to reach and serve.
2. **Value Propositions**: Describes the bundle of products and services that create value for a specific customer segment.
3. **Channels**: Outlines how a company communicates with and reaches its customer segments to deliver its value proposition.
4. **Customer Relationships**: Describes the types of relationships a company establishes with specific customer segments.
5. **Revenue Streams**: Represents the cash a company generates from each customer segment.
6. **Key Resources**: Describes the most important assets required to make a business model work.
7. **Key Activities**: Outlines the most important things a company must do to make its business model work.

8. **Key Partnerships**: Identifies the network of suppliers and partners that make the business model effective.

9. **Cost Structure**: Describes all costs incurred to operate a business model.

5.11.2 Application of the Business Model Canvas:
- **Startups and New Ventures**: Particularly useful for startups developing a business model from scratch or pivoting their existing model.
- **Established Businesses**: Helps larger companies in reassessing and innovating their existing business models or exploring new business opportunities.
- **Strategic Planning and Innovation**: Facilitates discussion, creativity, and analysis during strategic planning sessions and innovation workshops.

5.11.3 Advantages of the Canvas:
- **Flexibility and Simplicity**: Offers a simple, flexible, and dynamic framework that can be easily modified and adapted.
- **Visual and Collaborative Tool**: The visual nature of the canvas makes it an effective tool for collaborative discussions and brainstorming.
- **Holistic View**: Provides a holistic view of a business on a single canvas, facilitating a better understanding of the interconnections and the big picture.

5.11.4 Challenges and Considerations:
- **Oversimplification**: While simplicity is a strength, there is a risk of oversimplifying complex business models.
- **Dynamic Nature**: Business models are dynamic and the canvas should be revisited and revised regularly to reflect changes.

The Business Model Canvas is a powerful tool for entrepreneurs and business leaders to map out and understand their business models. It encourages a thorough yet straightforward approach to business planning and strategy, making it easier to pinpoint how value is created, delivered, and captured by an organization.

6 Innovation Processes and Methodologies

6.1 Basic Research and Development (Early 20th Century Onwards)

Basic Research and Development (R&D) has been a cornerstone of the innovation process since the early 20th century. It involves systematic investigation and exploration, primarily aimed at acquiring new knowledge. This process is fundamental in advancing scientific understanding and laying the groundwork for developing new products, technologies, or systems.

6.1.1 The R&D Process:

1. **Basic Research**: This is the initial stage, involving scientific research aimed at understanding fundamental principles. It's often curiosity-driven, without immediate commercial applications in mind.

2. **Applied Research**: This stage focuses on using the knowledge gained from basic research to solve specific problems or develop new products.

3. **Development**: The final stage involves the actual design and development of new products, processes, or technologies based on the findings of applied research.

6.1.2 Evolution of Basic R&D:

- **Early 20th Century**: The concept of organized R&D began to take shape in industrial settings, with companies establishing their own research labs to develop new technologies.

- **Post World War II**: The period saw a significant expansion in R&D activities, driven by both governmental and corporate investments, particularly in fields like aerospace, electronics, and pharmaceuticals.

- **Modern Era**: Today, R&D is a crucial part of many organizations, spanning diverse industries. The focus has expanded from not just developing new products but also improving existing ones and finding efficient processes.

6.1.3 Key Aspects of Basic R&D:

- **Exploratory Nature**: Basic R&D is often exploratory, delving into fundamental questions and seeking to uncover new knowledge without immediate commercial applications in mind.

- **Long-Term Investment**: Basic R&D typically requires long-term investment, given that the path from research to commercialization can be lengthy and uncertain.

- **Interdisciplinary Approach**: Modern R&D increasingly involves a multidisciplinary approach, integrating knowledge from various fields to foster innovation.

6.1.4 Examples and Impact:

- **Pharmaceuticals**: Basic R&D in pharmaceuticals has led to groundbreaking drugs, vaccines, and therapies, improving global health outcomes.

- **Technology and Electronics**: Fundamental research in electronics and materials science has been instrumental in advancements like semiconductors, leading to the digital revolution.

- **Environmental Science**: R&D in environmental science is crucial for developing sustainable technologies and addressing climate change.

6.1.5 Challenges in Basic R&D:

- **Funding and Resource Allocation**: Ensuring sustained funding for R&D can be challenging, especially for research with uncertain commercial prospects.

- **Balancing Commercial and Scientific Goals**: In corporate settings, aligning R&D activities with business objectives while maintaining the integrity of scientific exploration can be complex.

6.2 Brainstorming (1953)

Brainstorming, a method popularized by Alex Osborn in 1953, is a widely used technique in both business and education for generating creative ideas and solutions through group discussion. It encourages participants to come up with thoughts and ideas that can seem silly or outlandish, with the concept that such creative processes can lead to novel and useful solutions.

6.2.1 Development of Brainstorming:

- **Origins**: Alex Osborn, an advertising executive, introduced the concept of brainstorming in his book "Applied Imagination." He developed this technique based on his observation that traditional business meetings often inhibited the creation of new ideas.

- **Core Concept**: The fundamental principle of brainstorming is to generate as many ideas as possible in a judgment-free environment, fostering creativity and open-mindedness.

6.2.2 Principles and Process of Brainstorming:

1. **No Criticism**: Ideas are not criticized or evaluated during the brainstorming session to ensure that participants feel free to suggest any thought, no matter how unconventional.

2. **Welcome Wild Ideas**: Encourages out-of-the-box thinking and valuing unconventional and innovative ideas.

3. **Quantity Over Quality**: The focus is on generating a high volume of ideas, as it is believed that this would lead to high-quality concepts.

4. **Combination and Improvement of Ideas**: Encourages participants to build on or combine ideas generated by others, fostering collaborative thinking.

6.2.3 Applications of Brainstorming:

- **Problem-Solving**: Commonly used in business and educational settings to generate a broad range of ideas for problem-solving.

- **Product Development**: Used to generate innovative ideas for new products or improvements to existing products.

- **Creative Projects**: Employed in creative industries like advertising, design, and writing to develop fresh concepts and perspectives.

6.2.4 Benefits of Brainstorming:

- **Fostering Creativity and Innovation**: Provides a space for free thinking that can lead to unique and novel solutions.

- **Team Building**: Encourages collaboration and can strengthen team dynamics.

- **Engagement and Inclusion**: Allows all members of a group to contribute and have their ideas heard.

6.2.5 Challenges and Critiques of Brainstorming:
- **Idea Quality**: The emphasis on quantity can sometimes overshadow the need for practical and feasible ideas.
- **Groupthink**: There is a risk of groupthink, where the desire for harmony or conformity results in an irrational or dysfunctional decision-making outcome.
- **Dominance of Vocal Participants**: Often, more vocal participants can dominate the session, while introverts might not contribute as much.

Brainstorming remains a fundamental tool in the creative process, providing a structured yet open environment for generating a wealth of ideas. When facilitated effectively, it can unlock a team's creative potential and lead to innovative solutions that might not emerge through more conventional discussion methods.

6.3 BRAINWRITING IDEATION TECHNIQUE

Brainwriting is an alternative to traditional brainstorming, focusing on a quieter, more reflective approach to idea generation. It involves participants writing down their ideas independently before sharing them with the group, promoting a more inclusive and diverse ideation process.

6.3.1 How Brainwriting Works
- Participants are given a topic or problem and asked to write down their ideas on paper or post-it notes.
- After a set period, usually a few minutes, they pass their ideas to the next person, who builds upon them.
- This process continues until each participant has contributed to each idea.

6.3.2 Applications of Brainwriting
- **Product Development**: Generating innovative features or improvements for products.

- **Business Strategy**: Developing new strategies for market expansion, customer engagement, or operational efficiency.
- **Creative Projects**: Idea generation for marketing campaigns, design projects, or content creation.

6.3.3 Benefits of Brainwriting
- **Encourages Participation**: More introverted team members may feel more comfortable expressing their ideas in writing rather than speaking aloud.
- **Richer Idea Development**: Ideas are built upon iteratively, often leading to more well-developed concepts.
- **Reduces Dominance**: Prevents louder voices from dominating the conversation, ensuring a more equitable contribution from all participants.

6.3.4 Challenges in Implementing Brainwriting
- **Idea Saturation**: Participants might struggle with idea generation if the session goes on too long.
- **Group Dynamics**: The success of brainwriting can depend on the dynamics of the group and their comfort with sharing and building upon each other's ideas.

6.3.5 Best Practices for Brainwriting
- **Clear Instructions**: Ensure participants understand the process and the goal of the session.
- **Time Management**: Keep each round of idea passing brief to maintain energy and focus.
- **Post-Session Synthesis**: Allocate time to discuss and refine the ideas collectively after the writing rounds.

Brainwriting is an effective ideation technique that encourages diverse and thoughtful idea generation. It can lead to richer, more varied concepts than traditional brainstorming, making it a valuable tool in creative and strategic planning processes.

6.4 Reverse Brainstorming Ideation Technique

Reverse brainstorming is a creative problem-solving technique that inverts the traditional brainstorming process. Instead of directly seeking solutions to a problem, participants first explore all the ways to cause or worsen the problem. This counterintuitive approach often leads to innovative solutions by examining the problem from a different perspective.

6.4.1 How Reverse Brainstorming Works

- **Identify the Problem**: Clearly define the problem or challenge at hand.
- **Generate Reverse Ideas**: Brainstorm ideas on how to create or exacerbate the problem.
- **Invert the Ideas**: Flip these negative ideas into positive solutions.

6.4.2 Applications of Reverse Brainstorming

- **Product Development**: Identifying potential flaws or failures in a product to improve its design.
- **Service Improvement**: Exploring ways a service could disappoint customers to enhance customer satisfaction.
- **Process Optimization**: Finding potential inefficiencies or errors in a process to make it more efficient.

6.4.3 Benefits of Reverse Brainstorming

- **Overcomes Mental Blocks**: Helps in overcoming conventional thinking patterns that can hinder creative problem-solving.
- **Engages Critical Thinking**: Encourages participants to think critically and analytically.
- **Enhances Problem Understanding**: Provides a deeper understanding of the problem by examining it from different angles.

6.4.4 Examples of Reverse Brainstorming in Practice

1. **Customer Service Improvement**: A company might ask, "How can we make our customer service worse?" This could lead to insights about inefficiencies or areas where customers might be currently dissatisfied.

2. **Product Safety**: A toy manufacturer could explore ways a toy might be unsafe, leading to innovative design changes to enhance safety.

6.4.5 Challenges in Implementing Reverse Brainstorming
- **Participant Buy-In**: Some participants might find the negative focus initially off-putting or confusing.
- **Idea Conversion**: Effectively flipping negative ideas into positive solutions can be challenging.
- **Facilitation**: Requires a skilled facilitator to guide the discussion and keep the session productive.

6.4.6 Best Practices for Reverse Brainstorming
- **Clear Guidance**: Provide clear instructions and examples to participants on how the process works.
- **Positive Environment**: Maintain a positive and open environment, despite the negative nature of the brainstorming.
- **Focused Discussion**: Keep the discussion focused on the problem at hand to ensure relevant idea generation.

Reverse brainstorming is an effective technique for stimulating innovative thinking and problem-solving. By intentionally focusing on negative outcomes, it allows teams to uncover hidden problems and generate creative solutions that might not emerge through traditional brainstorming methods.

6.5 TRIZ (Theory of Inventive Problem Solving, 1956)

TRIZ, an acronym for Teoriya Resheniya Izobretatelskikh Zadach, translated as "Theory of Inventive Problem Solving," was developed by Soviet engineer and researcher Genrich Altshuller in 1956. It is a methodology, tool set, knowledge base, and model-based technology for generating innovative ideas and solutions for problem solving.

6.5.1 Development of TRIZ:
- **Historical Background**: Altshuller and his colleagues began studying patterns in the global patent literature to identify universal principles of invention. This study led to the creation of TRIZ.

- **Core Concept**: TRIZ is based on the principle that the evolution of systems is governed by certain laws, and by understanding these laws, inventors can deliberately and systematically create new innovations.

6.5.2 Key Principles of TRIZ:

1. **Problem Analysis and Ideality**: TRIZ encourages a deep analysis of the problem and the ideal state of the system without constraints.

2. **40 Inventive Principles and Contradiction Matrix**: It provides a structured way to think outside the box by applying these principles to overcome contradictions in a problem.

3. **Patterns of System Evolution**: TRIZ identifies patterns in the way technological systems evolve and uses these patterns to predict future developments and solutions.

4. **Use of Analogies**: Encourages solving problems by drawing analogies with problems solved in other areas or industries.

6.5.3 TRIZ Tools and Techniques:

- **Contradiction Matrix**: A tool for solving technical contradictions with standard solutions based on 39 parameters.

- **ARIZ (Algorithm for Inventive Problem Solving)**: A step-by-step procedure for systematically solving complex problems.

- **Function Analysis**: Understanding the relationships between different elements of a system.

6.5.4 Applications of TRIZ:

- **Innovation and Design**: Used in product design and engineering to develop new products and improve existing ones.

- **Business and Management**: Applied in organizational problem-solving and to innovate business processes.

- **Education and Research**: As a tool for teaching creative problem-solving and technical innovation.

6.5.5 Benefits of TRIZ:

- **Systematic Innovation**: Provides a systematic framework for creativity that increases the likelihood of breakthrough innovations.

- **Efficiency**: Helps to solve complex problems more efficiently by using proven principles and strategies.

- **Cross-Disciplinary**: Can be applied across various industries and fields, making it a versatile tool.

6.5.6 Challenges in Implementing TRIZ:
- **Learning Curve**: The methodology can be complex and may require substantial training to use effectively.

- **Cultural Adoption**: Implementing TRIZ often requires a shift in thinking and culture within an organization.

TRIZ stands out as a unique and powerful tool for systematic innovation and problem-solving. Its structured approach to creativity, based on the analysis of thousands of patents and inventions, provides a robust framework for individuals and organizations seeking to harness innovation systematically.

6.6 QUALITY CIRCLES PROCESS FOR INNOVATION (1962)

Introduction to Quality Circles: Originating in Japan in 1962, Quality Circles are a process of innovation and problem-solving developed in the manufacturing sector. They involve small groups of workers who perform similar tasks and meet regularly to identify, analyze, and solve work-related problems, typically focusing on product quality improvement.

6.6.1 Development and Spread of Quality Circles:
- **Japanese Origins**: Quality Circles were part of Japan's efforts to rebuild its industry post-World War II. They were inspired by American management techniques but adapted to fit the Japanese work culture.

- **Global Adoption**: In the 1970s and 1980s, the concept spread globally as companies sought to emulate the success of Japanese manufacturing.

6.6.2 Structure and Functioning of Quality Circles:
- **Group Composition**: Typically consist of 6-12 employees from the same work area who meet regularly.

- **Meetings and Activities**: Meetings are used to discuss problems, propose solutions, and plan improvements. These may include brainstorming sessions, data collection and analysis, and presentation of solutions to management.

- **Leadership**: Usually led by a supervisor or a democratically elected leader, with training provided to all members.

6.6.3 Principles Behind Quality Circles:

- **Employee Empowerment**: One of the fundamental principles is empowering workers by involving them in decision-making processes.
- **Collaboration**: Emphasizes teamwork and collaborative problem-solving.
- **Continuous Improvement**: Focuses on ongoing improvements (Kaizen), rather than one-time changes.

6.6.4 Benefits of Quality Circles:

- **Improved Quality and Productivity**: By tapping into the collective expertise of employees, quality circles can lead to improvements in product quality and operational efficiency.
- **Employee Motivation and Satisfaction**: Participation in quality circles can enhance job satisfaction, motivation, and a sense of ownership among employees.
- **Organizational Learning and Innovation**: Facilitates a culture of continuous learning and innovation at the grassroots level.

6.6.5 Challenges and Considerations:

- **Cultural Differences**: The effectiveness of quality circles can vary depending on organizational culture.
- **Sustained Commitment**: Requires ongoing commitment from both management and employees to be successful.

Quality Circles represent a significant innovation in organizational management, particularly in the context of manufacturing and production. By fostering a culture of continuous improvement and employee involvement, they not only enhance product quality but also contribute to employee engagement and organizational learning. As a process for innovation, quality circles demonstrate the value of collaborative problem-solving and grassroots initiatives.

6.7 Idea Campaigns Ideation Technique

Idea campaigns are a structured approach to gathering a large number of ideas within an organization or community, typically focused on a specific topic or challenge. This technique is part of open innovation, where input is solicited broadly to identify novel solutions and opportunities.

6.7.1 How Idea Campaigns Work

- **Define a Clear Objective**: Set a specific theme or challenge for the campaign.
- **Engage Participants**: Invite contributions from a wide range of participants, including employees, customers, or the public.
- **Collect Ideas**: Use platforms or events to gather ideas, ensuring easy participation.
- **Evaluate and Implement**: Review submissions, select the most promising ideas, and take steps toward implementation.

6.7.2 Applications of Idea Campaigns

- **Product Development**: Generating ideas for new products or features.
- **Process Improvement**: Identifying ways to enhance efficiency or effectiveness in operations.
- **Social Innovation**: Solving community or societal challenges through collaborative idea generation.

6.7.3 Benefits of Idea Campaigns

- **Diversity of Perspectives**: Draws on a wide range of viewpoints, leading to more innovative solutions.
- **Engagement and Buy-In**: Encourages stakeholder engagement and fosters a sense of ownership in the innovation process.
- **Scalability**: Can be scaled to suit different organizational sizes and types.

6.7.4 Examples of Idea Campaigns in Practice

1. **IBM's Innovation Jam**: IBM conducted a massive online brainstorming session, engaging over 150,000 participants worldwide to generate ideas for new technologies and business strategies.

2. **Starbucks' My Starbucks Idea**: An online platform where customers submit and vote on ideas for new products, services, and store improvements.

6.7.5 Challenges in Implementing Idea Campaigns
- **Quality of Submissions**: Managing the varying quality of submitted ideas.
- **Participant Engagement**: Encouraging active and widespread participation.
- **Resource Intensive**: Requires significant resources for moderation, evaluation, and follow-up.

6.7.6 Best Practices for Effective Idea Campaigns
- **Clear Communication**: Clearly communicate the purpose, guidelines, and expectations for the campaign.
- **Inclusive Participation**: Make the campaign accessible and inviting to a diverse group of participants.
- **Structured Review Process**: Have a robust process for reviewing and selecting ideas.

Idea campaigns are a powerful ideation technique for harnessing collective intelligence and creativity. By effectively organizing and managing these campaigns, organizations can tap into a wealth of ideas, driving innovation and fostering a culture of collaboration and engagement.

6.8 BROADCAST SEARCH IDEATION TECHNIQUE

Broadcast Search is an open innovation technique where a problem or challenge is broadcast to a wide audience to solicit solutions. Unlike traditional, closed R&D processes, this method taps into the collective intelligence and expertise of a diverse external group, often leading to more innovative and effective solutions.

6.8.1 How Broadcast Search Works
- **Define the Challenge**: Clearly articulate the problem or challenge that needs solving.

- **Broadcast to a Wide Audience**: Use various platforms to reach a broad and diverse audience, including industry experts, researchers, and the public.
- **Collect and Evaluate Solutions**: Gather submissions and evaluate them based on predefined criteria.
- **Implement and Reward**: Implement the best solutions and appropriately reward the contributors.

6.8.2 Applications of Broadcast Search
- **Scientific Problem-Solving**: Addressing complex scientific challenges that require specialized knowledge.
- **Product Innovation**: Generating innovative ideas for new products or improvements to existing ones.
- **Process Optimization**: Finding more efficient processes or solutions to operational challenges.

6.8.3 Benefits of Broadcast Search
- **Access to Diverse Expertise**: Taps into a wide range of skills and experiences beyond the organization's internal resources.
- **Speed and Efficiency**: Can lead to faster problem-solving compared to traditional methods.
- **Cost-Effectiveness**: Reduces the cost of R&D by leveraging external knowledge and creativity.

6.8.4 Examples of Broadcast Search in Practice
1. **Innocentive Challenges**: Innocentive is a platform that allows organizations to post challenges and solicit solutions from a global community of problem solvers.
2. **NASA's Challenges**: NASA frequently uses broadcast search techniques to solve complex space-related challenges by reaching out to the scientific community and the public.

6.8.5 Challenges in Implementing Broadcast Search
- **Quality Control**: Ensuring the quality and feasibility of the solutions provided by external contributors.

- **Intellectual Property Management**: Handling IP rights associated with externally sourced solutions.
- **Effective Communication**: Clearly communicating the problem in a way that is understandable to a broad audience.

6.8.6 Best Practices for Effective Broadcast Search
- **Clear and Concise Briefs**: Ensure the challenge is well-defined and communicated clearly.
- **Diverse Outreach**: Use multiple channels to reach a diverse audience.
- **Fair and Transparent Reward System**: Establish a clear and fair system for rewarding contributors.

Broadcast Search is a powerful ideation technique that leverages external expertise to solve complex problems. By effectively employing this technique, organizations can significantly enhance their innovation capacity, bringing in fresh perspectives and novel solutions from a global pool of talent.

6.9 SCAMPER Tool

The SCAMPER tool, introduced by Bob Eberle in 1971, is a creative thinking technique that guides users through a series of thought-provoking questions to generate new ideas or solutions. The acronym SCAMPER stands for Substitute, Combine, Adapt, Modify, Put to another use, Eliminate, and Reverse. It is a practical and versatile tool widely used in various fields to inspire creativity and innovation.

6.9.1 Development and Purpose of SCAMPER:
- **Educational Roots**: Initially developed as an educational tool to enhance creative thinking in students, SCAMPER has since been adopted by businesses, designers, and innovators.
- **Idea Generation**: The primary purpose of SCAMPER is to provide a structured way to think differently about a product, service, or process and to explore new possibilities.

6.9.2 How SCAMPER Works:
Each letter in SCAMPER prompts users to think about an object or situation from different perspectives:

1. **Substitute**: What elements can be substituted to improve the product or process?
2. **Combine**: Can different elements be combined to create something new?
3. **Adapt**: How can something be adapted or copied from something else?
4. **Modify**: How can the item be modified in terms of size, shape, or form?
5. **Put to another use**: Can the item be used for other purposes?
6. **Eliminate**: What parts or features can be eliminated or simplified?
7. **Reverse**: Can any elements be reversed or rearranged?

6.9.3 Applications of SCAMPER:
- **Product Development**: Assists in brainstorming improvements or innovations for existing products.
- **Process Improvement**: Helps in finding ways to streamline or enhance processes.
- **Problem-Solving**: Can be used to generate alternative solutions to a problem.

6.9.4 Benefits of SCAMPER:
- **Spurs Creativity**: Encourages out-of-the-box thinking by challenging existing assumptions.
- **Versatility**: Applicable to a wide range of contexts and industries.
- **Ease of Use**: Simple to understand and can be used individually or in group brainstorming sessions.

6.9.5 Challenges and Considerations:
- **Requires Open Mindset**: The effectiveness of SCAMPER is dependent on the user's willingness to explore and consider unconventional ideas.
- **Guidance for Productive Use**: May require facilitation or guidance, especially in group settings, to ensure productive and focused ideation sessions.

The SCAMPER tool is a valuable resource for anyone looking to enhance their creative thinking and problem-solving abilities. By systematically exploring different ways to improve or innovate, SCAMPER helps unlock new perspectives and potential solutions.

6.10 Crazy 8 Ideation Technique

Crazy 8s is a rapid ideation technique used in brainstorming sessions to generate a wide range of ideas in a short amount of time. It is particularly useful in design thinking and creative problem-solving processes.

6.10.1 How Crazy 8s Work

- Participants are given a sheet of paper divided into eight sections.
- They have eight minutes to generate eight distinct ideas, spending one minute on each.
- The focus is on quantity over quality, encouraging free-flowing creativity.

6.10.2 Applications of Crazy 8s

- **Product Development**: Generating diverse ideas for new product features or designs.
- **Marketing Campaigns**: Brainstorming various marketing strategies or campaign ideas.
- **Business Strategy**: Coming up with different approaches to address business challenges.

6.10.3 Examples of Crazy 8s in Action

1. **Mobile App Design**: A team brainstorming different user interface layouts or functionalities for a new app.
2. **Restaurant Promotions**: Chefs and managers brainstorming unique promotional ideas to attract more customers.

6.10.4 Benefits of the Crazy 8s Technique

- **Encourages Creativity**: The time limit and quantity goal push participants to think creatively and freely.

- **Inclusive Participation**: Everyone has an equal opportunity to contribute ideas.
- **Variety of Ideas**: Produces a broad range of ideas that can be further explored or combined.

6.10.5 Challenges in Implementing Crazy 8s
- **Time Constraint**: Some participants may find the time limit too restrictive.
- **Idea Quality**: The focus on quantity can sometimes lead to less feasible or relevant ideas.
- **Analysis Paralysis**: Participants may feel overwhelmed when choosing which ideas to develop further.

6.10.6 Best Practices for Crazy 8s
- **Clear Objective**: Start with a clear understanding of the problem or goal.
- **Encourage Openness**: Remind participants that there are no wrong ideas and encourage wild or unconventional thinking.
- **Post-Session Review**: Allocate time after the session to review and discuss the ideas generated.

The Crazy 8s ideation technique is a powerful tool in the creative process, enabling teams to quickly generate a diverse array of ideas. It's particularly beneficial in the early stages of a project when exploring a wide range of possibilities is crucial for innovative solutions.

6.11 Pyramid Search Ideation Technique
Pyramid Search is an innovative ideation technique that enables organizations to find novel solutions by tapping into knowledge beyond their immediate domain. Based on the principle that people with broad interests in a particular area tend to know others with higher levels of knowledge, this method is akin to how a doctor refers patients to specialists.

6.11.1 Application in Innovation Management
The pyramid search technique is particularly useful for R&D teams and innovation managers. It allows them to gather novel solutions in collaboration

with domain experts outside their organization, fostering a more open innovation approach.

6.11.2 Benefits of Pyramid Search

- **Expands Idea Horizons**: By reaching out to experts in various fields, teams can uncover unique solutions that might not be apparent within their own domain.

- **Reduces Local Search Biases**: Looking for ideas beyond the organization's walls prevents local search biases, enhancing the novelty and diversity of ideas generated.

6.11.3 Steps in the Pyramid Search Process

1. **Identifying Knowledgeable Individuals**: Begin by identifying people you believe have higher levels of knowledge about your problem or who can guide you to such individuals.

2. **Sequential Discussion**: Discuss the problem with these individuals, each leading you to others with more specific or advanced knowledge.

3. **Reaching the Top of the Pyramid**: Continue this process until you reach individuals ('the top of the pyramid') with the desired high levels of expertise who can provide the solutions you need.

6.11.4 Examples of Pyramid Search in Practice

1. **Procter & Gamble's Pringles Innovation**: P&G applied pyramid searching for its Pringles Potato Crisps, leading them to a professor in Bologna, Italy, who had invented a method to print edible images on cakes. This solution was adapted for printing images on Pringles crisps.

2. **Antilock Braking System (ABS)**: The ABS technology in cars was developed by looking for solutions in analogous markets, like the aircraft industry, which faced similar extreme braking needs.

3. **Medical Imaging Breakthroughs**: A team researching medical imaging used the technique to connect with radiologists and then pattern recognition experts, eventually leading them to military reconnaissance experts who had innovated high-resolution imaging using pattern recognition software.

6.11.5 Challenges in Implementing Pyramid Search
- **Finding the Right Contacts**: The initial step of identifying knowledgeable individuals can be challenging.
- **Ensuring Relevance**: Ensuring that the insights and solutions are relevant and applicable to the original problem.

6.11.6 Best Practices for Effective Pyramid Search
- **Diverse Networking**: Build a diverse network of contacts across various industries.
- **Open Mindset**: Approach the process with an open mind, ready to explore unconventional solutions.
- **Consistent Follow-Up**: Maintain communication with contacts to build a sustained knowledge-sharing network.

The Pyramid Search Ideation Technique is a powerful tool for driving innovation, particularly when traditional internal brainstorming fails to yield fresh solutions. By systematically reaching out to external experts and traversing different domains, organizations can uncover groundbreaking ideas and apply them to their unique challenges.

6.12 LEGO SERIOUS PLAY IDEATION TECHNIQUE
LEGO Serious Play (LSP) is an innovative, experiential process designed to enhance innovation and business performance. Originating from the LEGO Group, this technique uses LEGO bricks as a medium for storytelling and problem-solving, enabling participants to communicate more effectively and unleash creative thinking.

6.12.1 Principles of LEGO Serious Play
- **Hands-On, Minds-On Learning**: Encourages active participation and engagement through building models.
- **Storymaking and Sharing**: Uses storytelling to bring ideas and models to life.
- **Systemic Thinking**: Encourages thinking in systems and exploring complex relationships.

6.12.2 How LEGO Serious Play Works
- Participants are presented with a challenge or question.
- They build symbolic and metaphoric models using LEGO bricks to represent their thoughts, ideas, and reflections on the challenge.
- Participants share their models and the stories behind them with the group, fostering a deeper understanding of different perspectives.

6.12.3 Applications of LEGO Serious Play
- **Team Building**: Enhancing team collaboration and communication.
- **Strategy Development**: Exploring complex business strategies and scenarios.
- **Problem-Solving**: Addressing and finding creative solutions to business challenges.

6.12.4 Benefits of LEGO Serious Play
- **Encourages Creativity and Innovation**: Provides a playful, open environment that stimulates creativity.
- **Improves Communication**: Helps participants articulate thoughts and ideas that are hard to express with words alone.
- **Builds Shared Understanding**: Allows teams to see and understand different viewpoints and ideas.

6.12.5 Examples of LEGO Serious Play in Action
1. **Corporate Strategy Sessions**: Companies use LSP to explore future strategies, building models of different scenarios and their potential impacts.
2. **Team Development Workshops**: Teams build models representing team dynamics, challenges, and goals to foster better understanding and collaboration.
3. **Innovation Workshops**: Participants use LEGO bricks to build prototypes of new products or visualize solutions to complex problems.

6.12.6 Challenges in Implementing LEGO Serious Play

- **Facilitation Skill**: Requires skilled facilitators to guide the process and ensure productive outcomes.
- **Participant Buy-In**: Some participants may initially be skeptical of using a playful method in a serious business context.
- **Time-Intensive**: The process can be time-consuming, requiring ample time for building and discussion.

6.12.7 Best Practices for LEGO Serious Play

- **Skilled Facilitation**: Use experienced facilitators who understand how to guide the process effectively.
- **Clear Objectives**: Start with clear objectives and goals for what the session aims to achieve.
- **Encourage Openness**: Create a safe, open environment where participants feel comfortable sharing and building on each other's ideas.

LEGO Serious Play is a powerful tool for unlocking creativity, enhancing team dynamics, and exploring complex business issues. By tapping into the power of play, it allows participants to express ideas in a tangible and engaging way, leading to deeper insights and innovative solutions.

6.13 Nudging for Idea Generation

Nudging, a concept from behavioral economics, involves subtly guiding individuals towards desired behaviors without restricting their freedom of choice. In the context of innovation, nudging can be an effective tool for stimulating idea generation, encouraging creative thinking, and overcoming cognitive biases that hinder the ideation process.

6.13.1 How Nudging Works in Idea Generation

- **Environment Design**: Creating environments that foster creativity and open-minded thinking.
- **Choice Architecture**: Presenting options in a way that subtly influences the generation and selection of ideas.
- **Positive Reinforcement**: Using incentives and rewards to encourage participation and idea sharing.

6.13.2 Applications of Nudging in Innovation
- **Brainstorming Sessions**: Designing brainstorming sessions that nudge participants towards more creative and diverse thinking.
- **Innovation Workshops**: Structuring workshops to encourage collaboration and out-of-the-box thinking.
- **Employee Engagement**: Encouraging employees across the organization to contribute ideas and insights.

6.13.3 Benefits of Nudging for Idea Generation
- **Enhanced Creativity**: Nudges can break down barriers to creative thinking, leading to more innovative ideas.
- **Diversity of Ideas**: Helps in generating a wider range of ideas by preventing groupthink.
- **Increased Participation**: Encourages broader participation in the ideation process, tapping into collective intelligence.

6.13.4 Examples of Nudging in Idea Generation
1. **Designing Creative Spaces**: Companies like Google design their workspaces with creative nudges like playful decor and collaborative spaces to stimulate creative thinking.
2. **Idea Submission Platforms**: Online platforms that nudge employees to submit ideas by making the process easy, transparent, and rewarding.

6.13.5 Challenges in Implementing Nudging
- **Balance**: Finding the right balance between nudging and allowing freedom of thought.
- **Cultural Fit**: Ensuring that nudges are aligned with the organization's culture and values.
- **Measuring Effectiveness**: Quantifying the impact of nudges on idea generation can be challenging.

6.13.6 Best Practices for Nudging in Idea Generation
- **Subtlety**: Ensure that nudges are subtle and do not feel manipulative.
- **Customization**: Tailor nudges to fit the specific context and audience.

- **Ethical Considerations**: Be mindful of the ethical implications and ensure that nudges are used responsibly.

Nudging for idea generation is a nuanced approach that can significantly enhance the innovation process. By thoughtfully designing nudges, organizations can foster an environment conducive to creative thinking and idea sharing, leading to more innovative outcomes.

6.14 Voice of the Customer (VOC, 1980s)

Originating in the 1980s, Voice of the Customer (VOC) is a process for capturing customers' expectations, preferences, and aversions. It has become a cornerstone in market research and product development, helping companies align their products and services with customer needs.

6.14.1 Development and Purpose of VOC:

- **Roots in Quality Management**: VOC emerged from Total Quality Management (TQM) practices, where understanding customer requirements was key to improving product quality.
- **Focus on Customer Needs**: The primary goal of VOC is to gather detailed and structured information about customer requirements and use this data to inform decision-making in product development, service design, and marketing strategies.

6.14.2 VOC Process:

1. **Data Collection**: Involves gathering customer feedback through various methods like surveys, interviews, focus groups, and observation.
2. **Analysis and Interpretation**: The collected data is analyzed to extract insights about customer needs, both spoken and unspoken.
3. **Actionable Insights**: Translating the analysis into actionable product features, service enhancements, or customer experiences.
4. **Integration into Development**: Incorporating these insights into product development, service design, or marketing strategies.

6.14.3 Tools and Techniques:

- **Qualitative Research**: In-depth interviews and focus groups to understand customer attitudes, beliefs, and desires.

- **Quantitative Research**: Surveys and questionnaires that provide measurable data on customer preferences and behaviors.
- **Customer Journey Mapping**: Visualizing the customer's complete journey with a product or service to identify key touchpoints and opportunities for improvement.

6.14.4 Benefits of VOC:
- **Enhanced Customer Satisfaction**: By understanding and addressing customer needs, companies can improve customer satisfaction and loyalty.
- **Informed Product Development**: VOC helps ensure that new products or features align with what customers truly want.
- **Competitive Advantage**: Helps companies stay ahead of competitors by proactively responding to customer needs.

6.14.5 Challenges in Implementing VOC:
- **Complexity in Analysis**: Interpreting VOC data can be complex, requiring sophisticated analysis tools and expertise.
- **Bias and Misinterpretation**: There's a risk of bias in data collection or misinterpretation of customer feedback.
- **Integrating into Business Processes**: Effectively incorporating customer insights into business processes can be challenging.

Voice of the Customer is a vital process for any customer-centric organization. By systematically capturing and analyzing customer feedback, companies can make informed decisions that enhance the customer experience and drive innovation. As markets become increasingly competitive, the ability to accurately and effectively understand and respond to the voice of the customer becomes more crucial than ever.

6.15 Stage-Gate Process (Cooper, 1980s)

The Stage-Gate Process, developed by Dr. Robert G. Cooper in the 1980s, represents a project management approach that has become a fundamental part of new product development across various industries. This method structures the process of guiding a new product from the idea stage through to its launch and beyond, using a phased approach.

6.15.1 Fundamentals of the Stage-Gate Process:
- **Structured Framework**: The process divides the journey of new product development into distinct stages, each separated by decision points known as gates.
- **Stages**: Each stage consists of a set of prescribed activities aimed at gathering the information necessary to progress to the next stage. These stages typically include scoping, business case development, development, testing, and validation, followed by product launch.
- **Gates**: Gates are decision points where stakeholders review the project's progress and decide whether to continue, modify, or halt the project. Criteria at these gates typically include technical feasibility, market attractiveness, and financial viability.

6.15.2 Application of the Stage-Gate Process:
- **Risk Management**: By breaking the project into stages and evaluating at each gate, the process helps manage risk by avoiding uncontrolled progression of flawed projects.
- **Resource Allocation**: Allows for effective allocation and reallocation of resources at each stage, ensuring efficient use of capital and manpower.

6.15.3 Examples of Stage-Gate in Action:
- **Consumer Goods**: Many consumer goods companies implement the Stage-Gate Process to manage the development of new products, from ideation through market testing and launch.
- **Pharmaceuticals**: In the pharmaceutical industry, this process aligns with regulatory milestones, guiding drugs from initial discovery through clinical trials to market approval.

6.15.4 Advantages and Limitations:
- **Clarity and Control**: Provides a clear roadmap for development and enables better control over the process, helping to align teams and objectives.

- **Flexibility**: While structured, it can be adapted to fit the size and scope of various projects.

- **Potential for Bureaucracy**: One critique of the model is that it may lead to a bureaucratic and inflexible process, potentially stifling creativity and responsiveness.

The Stage-Gate Process has become a cornerstone in new product development, offering a practical, structured approach that can significantly enhance the chances of a product's success in the market. While it is not without its critiques, its benefits in terms of risk management, clarity, and systematic progression make it a valuable tool in the arsenal of project and product managers.

6.16 AGILE DEVELOPMENT (2001)

Agile Development, originating in the software development industry in 2001 with the publication of the Agile Manifesto, represents a paradigm shift in how products are developed and delivered. It emphasizes iterative progress, team collaboration, customer feedback, and flexibility to adapt to changing requirements.

6.16.1 Foundations of Agile Development:

- **Agile Manifesto**: The foundation of Agile Development is the Agile Manifesto, which outlines key values and principles like individuals and interactions over processes and tools, working software over comprehensive documentation, customer collaboration over contract negotiation, and responding to change over following a plan.

- **Iterative and Incremental Approach**: Unlike traditional waterfall methodologies, Agile focuses on iterative development, where requirements and solutions evolve through collaborative effort.

6.16.2 Key Principles of Agile Development:

1. **Customer Satisfaction through Early and Continuous Delivery**: Delivering functional products or features to customers in a shorter timescale.

2. **Embrace Change**: Being open to and responding quickly to changes in requirements, even late in the development process.

3. **Frequent Delivery**: Producing working versions of the final product frequently, from a couple of weeks to a couple of months.
4. **Collaboration**: Daily cooperation between business stakeholders and developers throughout the project.
5. **Supportive Environment**: Building projects around motivated individuals and providing them with the environment and support they need.
6. **Face-to-Face Conversation**: Using direct communication as the most effective method for conveying information.
7. **Sustainable Development**: Maintaining a constant pace and avoiding burnout.
8. **Technical Excellence**: Continuous attention to technical excellence and good design enhances agility.
9. **Simplicity**: Focusing on what is necessary and cutting out unnecessary work.
10. **Self-Organizing Teams**: The best architectures, requirements, and designs emerge from self-organizing teams.
11. **Reflection and Adjustment**: Regularly reflecting on how to become more effective and adjusting behavior accordingly.

6.16.3 Applications of Agile Development:

- **Beyond Software**: While originating in software, Agile principles have been adapted for use in other types of projects and industries, including marketing, project management, and product development.
- **Scrum and Kanban**: Popular frameworks like Scrum and Kanban are used to implement Agile principles in practical settings.

6.16.4 Benefits and Challenges:

- **Flexibility and Responsiveness**: Agile allows teams to be more responsive to customer feedback and changing market conditions.
- **Improved Product Quality**: Regular testing and revisions lead to higher quality products.

- **Challenges**: Implementing Agile requires a cultural shift in many organizations and can be challenging in environments that are used to traditional hierarchical structures.

Agile Development has revolutionized the way teams approach project management and product development, offering a flexible and responsive framework that is particularly well-suited to the fast-paced and constantly evolving modern business environment. Its emphasis on customer collaboration, iterative development, and team empowerment has made it an essential methodology in various industries.

6.17 Design Thinking (2008)

Design Thinking emerged as a formal methodology in 2008, although its roots trace back much earlier. It's a solution-based approach to solving complex problems that are ill-defined or unknown. Popularized by design firm IDEO and the Stanford d.school, Design Thinking combines empathy for the context of a problem, creativity in generating insights and solutions, and rationality to analyze and fit solutions to the context.

6.17.1 Core Elements of Design Thinking:

- **Human-Centric**: At its core, Design Thinking is deeply human-centric, focusing on understanding people for whom products or services are being designed.

- **Iterative Process**: The process is iterative, involving repeated brainstorming, prototyping, testing, and refining ideas and solutions.

- **Five Phases**: The methodology is often divided into five phases – Empathize, Define, Ideate, Prototype, and Test. However, these are not necessarily sequential and can occur in parallel or be repeated iteratively.

6.17.2 Phases of Design Thinking:

1. **Empathize**: Understanding the human needs involved, through observation, engagement, and empathizing with people to understand their experiences and motivations.

2. **Define**: Framing the problem and defining the problem space based on insights gained during the empathy phase.

3. **Ideate**: Generating a range of possible solutions through brainstorming and other ideation techniques.
4. **Prototype**: Building a representation of one or more of the ideas to show to others and test its feasibility.
5. **Test**: Employing a trial-and-error approach, using feedback to refine solutions.

6.17.3 Applications of Design Thinking:
- **Product and Service Design**: Widely used in developing new and innovative products and services that deeply resonate with users.
- **Business Strategy**: Applied to rethinking and innovating business models and strategies.
- **Social and Environmental Challenges**: Addressing complex social and environmental issues through a human-centric approach.

6.17.4 Benefits of Design Thinking:
- **Innovative Solutions**: Encourages out-of-the-box thinking, often leading to more innovative solutions.
- **Improved User Experience**: By focusing on the end-user, solutions are often more user-friendly and meet real needs more effectively.
- **Enhanced Collaboration**: Fosters collaboration across disciplines and stakeholders, leading to richer solutions.

6.17.5 Challenges in Implementing Design Thinking:
- **Mindset Shift**: Requires a shift in mindset to embrace ambiguity and a non-linear process.
- **Time and Resources**: Can be time-consuming and resource-intensive, particularly in the empathy and prototype stages.

Design Thinking has become an invaluable tool in the innovator's toolkit, offering a framework for approaching complex problems in a methodical yet creative way. Its emphasis on empathy, collaboration, and iterative learning makes it particularly effective in today's fast-paced, user-centered, and collaborative environment.

6.18 Lean Canvas (2010)

The Lean Canvas, adapted from the Business Model Canvas by Ash Maurya in 2010, is tailored specifically for startups and entrepreneurial ventures. It serves as a one-page business plan template that helps founders deconstruct their startup idea into key assumptions, replacing elaborate business plans with a concise, flexible, and actionable model.

6.18.1 Structure of the Lean Canvas:

The Lean Canvas is divided into nine segments, each focusing on critical aspects of a startup's business model:

1. **Problem**: Outlines the top problems or needs that the startup aims to address.

2. **Customer Segments**: Identifies the target audience or market for the solution.

3. **Unique Value Proposition**: Describes the compelling message that makes the solution stand out in the market.

4. **Solution**: Details the primary features or services that address the problems identified.

5. **Channels**: Explains how the startup will reach its customer segments.

6. **Revenue Streams**: Identifies how the startup will make money from its solutions.

7. **Cost Structure**: Lists the significant costs involved in operating the business.

8. **Key Metrics**: Defines the key indicators that will be used to measure the success of the business.

9. **Unfair Advantage**: Describes what gives the startup a competitive edge that cannot be easily replicated or bought.

6.18.2 Purpose and Application of Lean Canvas:

- **Focus on Key Factors**: Lean Canvas forces entrepreneurs to focus on and articulate the most critical factors for their business's success.

- **Rapid Hypothesis Testing**: Encourages quick testing and validation or refutation of business hypotheses.
- **Iterative Process**: Supports an iterative approach to business modeling, enabling entrepreneurs to quickly pivot or refine their strategies based on feedback and learning.

6.18.3 Benefits of Lean Canvas:
- **Clarity and Efficiency**: Provides a clear and straightforward way to articulate and test business ideas.
- **Adaptability**: Easily adaptable to changes, making it suitable for the dynamic nature of startups.
- **Communication Tool**: Acts as an effective communication tool for conveying the essence of a business to potential investors, partners, and team members.

6.18.4 Challenges in Using Lean Canvas:
- **Simplification Risks**: The simplification required to fit into the Lean Canvas can sometimes overlook complexities or subtleties of the business.
- **Regular Updating**: As the business evolves, the Lean Canvas needs to be continually updated to reflect changes.

The Lean Canvas is an invaluable tool for entrepreneurs, providing a clear and concise framework for developing and communicating their business ideas. By focusing on key aspects and enabling rapid iteration, the Lean Canvas helps startups navigate the uncertain journey of turning an idea into a viable business.

6.19 VALUE PROPOSITION CANVAS (2012)

Developed by Alexander Osterwalder in 2012, the Value Proposition Canvas is a tool designed to ensure that a product or service fits what the customer values and needs. It complements the Business Model Canvas by zooming in on two key elements of the latter: the value proposition and the customer segments.

6.19.1 Understanding the Value Proposition Canvas:
The Canvas is divided into two sections, each focusing on different aspects of the product-customer relationship:

1. **Customer Segment**: This section involves understanding the customer's world. It is broken down into three parts:

    - **Customer Jobs**: What tasks customers are trying to accomplish, problems they are trying to solve, or needs they wish to satisfy.
    - **Pains**: Negative experiences, emotions, and risks that customers face in the process of accomplishing these jobs.
    - **Gains**: The outcomes and benefits the customers want to achieve.

2. **Value Proposition**: This section maps out how the product or service creates value. It also has three parts:

    - **Products and Services**: The list of products and services the business offers.
    - **Pain Relievers**: How the product alleviates customer pains.
    - **Gain Creators**: How the product creates gains for the customer.

6.19.2 Using the Value Proposition Canvas:

- **Fit Between Product and Customer**: The central goal is to achieve a product-market fit, where the value proposition matches the customer's needs and wants.
- **Customer-Centric Approach**: It requires a deep understanding of the customer, allowing businesses to tailor their products or services to what the customer truly values.
- **Iterative Process**: As with many design thinking tools, developing a value proposition is an iterative process, involving constant testing and refinement based on customer feedback.

6.19.3 Applications and Benefits:

- **Product Development**: Useful in developing new products or refining existing ones.
- **Marketing and Sales**: Helps in crafting marketing messages and sales strategies that resonate with the target audience.

- **Strategic Business Decisions**: Assists in making strategic decisions about which customer segments to target and how.

6.19.4 Challenges and Considerations:
- **Complex Customer Understanding**: Requires an in-depth and often complex understanding of customer behaviors and needs.
- **Dynamic Markets**: Customer needs and the business environment can change rapidly, necessitating frequent updates to the canvas.

The Value Proposition Canvas is a powerful tool that focuses on ensuring the alignment of a product or service with the customer's needs, pains, and gains. It is an essential tool for businesses looking to develop products that truly resonate with their target market and achieve a strong market fit.

6.20 CROWDSOURCING (EARLY 2000S ONWARDS)

Crowdsourcing, a term coined in the early 2000s, refers to the practice of obtaining ideas, services, or content by soliciting contributions from a large group of people, particularly from online communities. It represents a significant shift in the way organizations and individuals gather information, solve problems, and complete tasks, leveraging the collective intelligence of a broad audience.

6.20.1 Development of Crowdsourcing:
- **Digital Era Emergence**: Crowdsourcing emerged as a popular method in the early 2000s, facilitated by the growth of the internet and social media platforms, which provided easy access to large groups of people.
- **Expansion Across Fields**: While initially used primarily in the technology sector, crowdsourcing has since expanded to various fields, including science, arts, and funding.

6.20.2 Mechanics of Crowdsourcing:
1. **Open Call**: An organization or individual issues an open call for contributions or solutions to a particular problem or task.
2. **Diverse Participation**: People from various backgrounds and with different skill sets contribute their ideas or skills.

3. **Aggregation and Selection**: Contributions are then aggregated and reviewed, with the best ideas or solutions being selected for implementation or further development.

6.20.3 Applications of Crowdsourcing:
- **Idea Generation**: Companies use crowdsourcing for brainstorming and idea generation, tapping into a wider range of perspectives.
- **Content Creation**: Media and publishing companies solicit content (such as articles, designs, or videos) from the public.
- **Crowdfunding**: Platforms like Kickstarter allow startups and projects to raise funds directly from the public.
- **Problem-Solving**: Scientific and research organizations use crowdsourcing to solve complex problems by gathering diverse inputs.

6.20.4 Benefits of Crowdsourcing:
- **Access to Diverse Ideas**: Crowdsourcing can gather a broad range of ideas and solutions from a diverse audience.
- **Cost-Effectiveness**: It can be more cost-effective than traditional methods of hiring professionals or consultants.
- **Community Engagement**: Helps in building a community around a brand or project, increasing engagement and loyalty.

6.20.5 Challenges in Crowdsourcing:
- **Quality Control**: Ensuring the quality of contributions can be challenging due to the variability in the expertise and seriousness of participants.
- **Intellectual Property Issues**: Managing and protecting intellectual property rights in a crowdsourcing context can be complex.
- **Overreliance on External Input**: Relying too heavily on crowdsourcing can lead to a lack of internal development and expertise.

Crowdsourcing represents a paradigm shift in how problems are solved and tasks are completed in the digital age. By leveraging the collective knowledge and creativity of a wide audience, organizations can find innovative solutions, engage with their community, and accomplish tasks more efficiently and effectively.

6.21 Frugal Innovation (2010s)

Frugal Innovation, gaining prominence in the 2010s, is a concept that focuses on reducing the complexity and cost of goods and services. Aimed at providing affordable and accessible solutions, particularly to those at the lower end of the economic pyramid, this approach is about doing more with less. It combines resourcefulness, cost-reduction, and sustainability, and is especially relevant in developing economies where resources are limited.

6.21.1 Development of Frugal Innovation:

- **Emergence in Developing Markets**: Initially observed in countries like India and China, Frugal Innovation emerged as a response to the need for affordable solutions in markets with limited resources and low consumer purchasing power.
- **Global Relevance**: The approach has since gained global relevance as businesses and societies increasingly seek sustainable and cost-effective solutions.

6.21.2 Principles of Frugal Innovation:

1. **Simplicity and Affordability**: Focuses on simplicity in design and affordability in pricing.
2. **Resource Efficiency**: Emphasizes making optimal use of available resources and minimizing waste.
3. **Customer-Centric**: Involves a deep understanding of the target customers' needs and constraints.
4. **Sustainability**: Integrates environmentally sustainable practices in the development process.
5. **Localized Solutions**: Tailors products and services to meet the specific needs of local markets and communities.

6.21.3 Applications and Examples:

- **Healthcare**: Portable, low-cost medical devices designed for remote or resource-limited settings.
- **Consumer Goods**: Simple, durable, and low-cost products tailored for emerging markets.

- **Financial Services**: Affordable, accessible banking and insurance products for the unbanked population.

6.21.4 Benefits of Frugal Innovation:
- **Social Impact**: Addresses the needs of underserved populations, providing access to essential goods and services.
- **Business Opportunities**: Opens new markets and business opportunities in emerging economies.
- **Sustainability**: Promotes sustainable practices by using fewer resources and reducing waste.

6.21.5 Challenges in Implementing Frugal Innovation:
- **Balancing Cost and Quality**: Maintaining quality while significantly reducing costs can be challenging.
- **Understanding Local Markets**: Requires a deep understanding of the local context and customer needs.
- **Scalability**: Scaling frugal innovations can be challenging, especially when moving beyond local markets.

Frugal Innovation represents a paradigm shift in how products and services are developed, focusing on affordability, simplicity, and sustainability. It challenges traditional notions of innovation by demonstrating that significant value can be created with limited resources, making it especially relevant in today's cost-conscious and environmentally aware global market.

7 Popular Concepts and Notion about Innovation

7.1 The Innovator's Dilemma

The Innovator's Dilemma is a concept popularized by Harvard Business School Professor Clayton Christensen in his 1997 book titled "The Innovator's Dilemma: When New Technologies Cause Great Firms to Fail." It addresses the challenge that established companies face when dealing with disruptive innovations that fundamentally change market dynamics.

7.1.1 Understanding The Innovator's Dilemma

The dilemma arises when established companies focus on improving products and services for their most demanding customers, leading to the overlooking of newer, often simpler and more affordable technologies that eventually disrupt the market.

7.1.2 Key Aspects of The Innovator's Dilemma

- **Disruptive vs. Sustaining Technology**: Disruptive technologies often start as cheaper, simpler options and gradually evolve, whereas sustaining technologies are improvements that incumbents make to existing products.

- **Market Leadership and Rigidity**: Market leaders may become rigid, focusing heavily on their most profitable segments and ignoring emerging markets or technologies.

- **Customer-Centric vs. Market-Centric**: Companies often prioritize customer requests for improvements, missing out on broader market needs and potential disruptions.

7.1.3 Examples of The Innovator's Dilemma

1. **Kodak's Downfall**: Kodak focused on improving film photography and underestimated the potential of digital photography, eventually leading to its decline.

2. **Blockbuster vs. Netflix**: Blockbuster, a giant in the video rental industry, failed to recognize the shift towards streaming services, leading to its fall and Netflix's rise.

7.1.4 Strategies to Overcome The Innovator's Dilemma
- **Fostering Innovation Culture**: Encourage risk-taking and exploration of new ideas that may seem unrelated or unprofitable initially.
- **Separate Teams for Disruptive Technologies**: Create independent teams dedicated to exploring potential disruptive technologies.
- **Customer Diversity**: Look beyond current customer demands to understand broader market trends and latent needs.

7.1.5 Challenges in Addressing The Innovator's Dilemma
- **Resource Allocation**: Balancing investment in current products versus potentially disruptive technologies.
- **Organizational Inertia**: Established companies often have set processes and cultures resistant to change.
- **Market Predictability**: Difficulty in predicting which innovations will truly be disruptive.

7.1.6 Best Practices in Responding to The Innovator's Dilemma
- **Continuous Market Research**: Stay informed about emerging technologies and market shifts.
- **Embrace Experimentation**: Adopt a mindset of experimentation and accept that not all initiatives will succeed.
- **Strategic Flexibility**: Be prepared to rapidly shift strategies in response to emerging disruptive technologies.

The Innovator's Dilemma highlights a critical challenge in business strategy and innovation management. Understanding and addressing this dilemma is essential for established companies to remain competitive in the face of disruptive innovations. It requires a balance of maintaining current business success while being agile and open to exploring and adopting new technologies and business models.

7.2 The 70-20-10 Rule of Innovation

The 70-20-10 rule is an innovation management principle suggesting how companies should allocate resources and focus to drive effective innovation. This model posits that 70% of efforts should be dedicated to core business activities, 20% to adjacent innovations, and 10% to new, transformative activities.

7.2.1 Understanding the 70-20-10 Allocation

1. **Core Innovation (70%)**: This segment focuses on innovations that improve existing products and services for existing customers. It's about optimizing current offerings and processes.

2. **Adjacent Innovation (20%)**: These efforts involve expanding from existing business into new areas. This could mean new products for current customers or current products for new markets.

3. **Transformational Innovation (10%)**: This small but critical portion is reserved for developing breakthroughs and new business models. These are higher-risk endeavors with the potential for significant returns.

7.2.2 Importance of the 70-20-10 Rule

- **Balanced Focus**: Ensures a balanced portfolio of innovation initiatives, from safe bets to more risky, high-reward projects.
- **Sustainable Growth**: Aims for steady growth with core innovations while seeking new growth opportunities through adjacent and transformational efforts.
- **Risk Management**: Distributes risk across a spectrum of initiatives.

7.2.3 Application in Business Strategy

Implementing the 70-20-10 rule requires careful planning and resource allocation. It also involves fostering a culture that supports different types of innovation, from incremental improvements to radical ideas.

7.2.4 Examples of the 70-20-10 Rule

1. **Google**: Known for its 70-20-10 approach, Google allocates resources to core business (like search and advertising), adjacent areas (like Android and Chrome), and transformational projects (like self-driving cars).

2. **3M**: A proponent of the rule, 3M applies it by investing in core products, adjacent markets with new applications of existing technologies, and transformational innovation like their renewable energy division.

7.2.5 Challenges in Implementing 70-20-10

- **Resource Allocation**: Appropriately distributing resources and attention across the three areas can be challenging.

- **Balancing Innovation and Operation**: Ensuring that the focus on innovation does not detract from core business operations.

- **Measuring Success**: Tracking progress and success across diverse types of innovation activities.

7.2.6 Best Practices for the 70-20-10 Rule

- **Clear Definition of Categories**: Clearly define what constitutes core, adjacent, and transformational innovation within the organization.

- **Supportive Leadership**: Leadership must support all types of innovation and understand the different metrics of success for each.

- **Encourage Cross-Pollination**: Ideas and learnings from one category can often benefit others, fostering an integrated approach to innovation.

The 70-20-10 rule of innovation is a framework that helps organizations balance their innovation portfolio across immediate improvements, medium-term growth opportunities, and long-term transformative bets. When implemented effectively, it can drive sustainable growth, diversify risk, and foster a robust culture of innovation.

7.3 THE THREE HORIZON INNOVATION FRAMEWORK

The Three Horizon Innovation Framework is a strategic model that helps businesses plan for sustainable growth by managing innovation across three time horizons. Developed by McKinsey & Company, this framework encourages organizations to think simultaneously about current performance and long-term goals.

7.3.1 Understanding the Three Horizons
1. **Horizon 1 - Core Business (Short-Term)**: Focuses on innovations that improve the current core business. These are typically incremental improvements to existing products, services, and processes.
2. **Horizon 2 - Emerging Opportunities (Medium-Term)**: Involves identifying and developing emerging opportunities that have the potential to become new revenue streams. These are often adjacent to the core business.
3. **Horizon 3 - Future Business (Long-Term)**: Encourages the exploration of completely new opportunities and business models that will define the future of the organization.

7.3.2 Purpose and Importance of the Framework
- **Balanced Innovation Portfolio**: Ensures a balance between focusing on current performance and investing in future growth.
- **Risk Management**: Spreads the risk across short-term, medium-term, and long-term initiatives.
- **Future-Proofing**: Helps organizations prepare for and shape their future rather than just reacting to it.

7.3.3 Application in Business Strategy
- **Resource Allocation**: Guides how to allocate resources, including capital, talent, and time, across different types of innovation initiatives.
- **Strategic Planning**: Offers a structure for strategic planning discussions, enabling a holistic view of the innovation pipeline.

7.3.4 Examples of the Three Horizon Framework
1. **Horizon 1 – Automotive Manufacturers**: Continuous improvements in current car models, such as fuel efficiency or safety features.
2. **Horizon 2 – Financial Services**: Banks developing mobile banking services as an extension of their traditional banking business.
3. **Horizon 3 – Tech Companies**: Investment in research and development of artificial intelligence or quantum computing, which could lead to new business models in the future.

7.3.5 Challenges in Implementing the Framework
- **Resource Competition**: Balancing the allocation of resources between immediate business needs and future opportunities.
- **Strategic Focus**: Maintaining focus on Horizon 3 initiatives, which may not provide immediate financial returns.
- **Cultural Adaptation**: Creating a culture that values long-term, exploratory innovation alongside short-term goals.

7.3.6 Best Practices for Utilizing the Three Horizon Framework
- **Leadership Commitment**: Strong leadership support for innovation across all three horizons.
- **Regular Review and Adjustment**: Regularly review progress across each horizon and adjust strategies as needed.
- **Cross-Functional Teams**: Leverage diverse, cross-functional teams for different horizon projects to encourage broad thinking and innovation.

The Three Horizon Innovation Framework is a powerful tool for strategic planning, allowing organizations to balance the demands of running a successful business today while actively preparing for the future. It fosters a culture of continuous innovation, ensuring long-term sustainability and growth.

7.4 Jobs-to-be-Done
Jobs-to-be-Done (JTBD) is a theory and framework for understanding customer needs and motivations in business and innovation. Developed and popularized by Harvard Business School professor Clayton Christensen, JTBD centers on the idea that consumers "hire" products or services to get specific jobs done.

7.4.1 Essence of the JTBD Framework
- **Understanding Customer Needs**: JTBD shifts the focus from the product to the underlying customer need or problem.
- **Functional and Emotional Jobs**: It recognizes that customers have both functional (practical) and emotional (psychological) jobs that they are looking to address.
- **Context-Driven**: Emphasizes the importance of the context in which a job arises.

7.4.2 JTBD in Action: Process and Application
1. **Identify the Job**: Determine what fundamental problem or need the customer is trying to address.
2. **Understand the Job Context**: Explore the specific circumstances in which the job arises.
3. **Design Solutions**: Develop products or services that are tailored to do the job effectively.
4. **Iterate Based on Feedback**: Continuously improve the solution based on customer feedback and changing needs.

7.4.3 Examples of Jobs-to-be-Done
1. **McDonald's Milkshake**: In a famous case study, Christensen found that customers "hired" milkshakes for two main jobs: to stay engaged during long, boring commutes and to satiate small children. This insight helped McDonald's tailor its product and marketing strategy.
2. **Uber**: Customers hire Uber for more than just transportation; they want convenience, safety, and control over their travel experience.
3. **Apple iPod**: Initially, customers hired the iPod to store and play music in a portable, user-friendly format, a job previously done by CD players and MP3 devices.

7.4.4 Challenges in Applying JTBD
- **Correctly Identifying the Job**: Misinterpreting the job can lead to developing the wrong solution.
- **Balancing Jobs**: Often, there are multiple jobs a product could address, and prioritizing them can be challenging.
- **Evolving Jobs**: As markets and technologies evolve, the nature of jobs can change, requiring ongoing adaptation.

7.4.5 Best Practices for Utilizing JTBD
- **Deep Customer Engagement**: Engage with customers through interviews and observations to uncover the real jobs.
- **Cross-Functional Collaboration**: Collaborate across departments (e.g., marketing, R&D, sales) to develop a holistic understanding of the job.

- **Continuous Learning and Adaptation**: Be open to learning and evolving your understanding of the job and how your product or service fulfills it.

The Jobs-to-be-Done framework provides a powerful lens for understanding customer needs and motivations. By focusing on the job and the context in which it arises, businesses and innovators can create more targeted, effective, and successful products and services.

7.5 Build-Measure-Learn

The Build-Measure-Learn loop is a core component of the Lean Startup methodology, introduced by Eric Ries. It's a framework that helps startups and businesses develop products and services in a more efficient and iterative manner by building a minimum viable product (MVP), measuring its effectiveness in the market, and learning from the results to make necessary adjustments.

7.5.1 Understanding the Build-Measure-Learn Loop

1. **Build**: Create a minimum viable product (MVP) – the simplest version of the product that allows the team to start the learning process as quickly as possible.

2. **Measure**: Collect data on how the MVP performs in the real world. This involves tracking user engagement, feedback, and other relevant metrics.

3. **Learn**: Analyze the data collected to gain insights. Decide whether to pivot (make a fundamental change in the product) or persevere (continue improving the current product).

7.5.2 Importance of the Build-Measure-Learn Loop

- **Rapid Feedback Cycle**: Enables quick learning about the market and user needs.

- **Risk Reduction**: Minimizes the risk of developing products that users don't want.

- **Efficient Resource Use**: Ensures resources are not wasted on features or products that won't succeed in the market.

7.5.3 Examples of Build-Measure-Learn in Action

1. **Dropbox**: Dropbox's initial MVP was a simple video demonstrating the product concept, which helped gauge user interest and gather feedback before developing the full application.

2. **Zappos**: The founder tested the online sale of shoes by posting shoe photos on a website without inventory. He bought the shoes from stores when orders came in, testing the market before building a full-fledged e-commerce business.

7.5.4 Challenges in Implementing Build-Measure-Learn

- **Identifying the Right Metrics**: Selecting which data to measure can be challenging but is crucial for meaningful insights.
- **Bias in Data Interpretation**: Avoiding confirmation bias and accurately interpreting the data to make informed decisions.
- **Balancing Speed and Quality**: Moving quickly through the loop without compromising the quality of the product or the learnings.

7.5.5 Best Practices for Effective Build-Measure-Learn Implementation

- **Focus on Learning Goals**: Define what you need to learn from each iteration.
- **Effective MVP Design**: Ensure the MVP is simple yet capable of testing the hypothesis.
- **Objective Data Analysis**: Analyze data objectively and be ready to pivot if necessary.
- **Iterative Approach**: Continuously iterate based on learnings to gradually build a product that meets market needs.

The Build-Measure-Learn loop is a vital process for startups and established businesses alike. It fosters a culture of experimentation and learning, essential for innovation in fast-paced and uncertain markets. By effectively implementing this loop, businesses can develop products that truly resonate with their target audience.

7.6 Minimum Viable Product (MVP)

The concept of the Minimum Viable Product (MVP) is central to the Lean Startup methodology developed by Eric Ries. An MVP is the simplest version of a product that can be released to customers. The purpose of an MVP is to test, learn, and iterate based on actual customer feedback with the least effort and cost.

7.6.1 Purpose and Importance of an MVP

- **Rapid Feedback and Learning**: MVPs allow companies to understand customer needs and reactions without fully developing the product.
- **Reduced Development Costs**: It helps in minimizing the resources spent on products that might not meet market needs.
- **Risk Mitigation**: Early and incremental releases reduce the risk of market failure.

7.6.2 Characteristics of a Good MVP

- **Sufficient to Fulfill the Core Purpose**: An MVP should deliver the fundamental value proposition of the product.
- **Testable**: It should be robust enough to be tested and provide valid learnings.
- **Iterative**: Designed to evolve based on user feedback.

7.6.3 Process of Developing an MVP

1. **Identify the Core Value Proposition**: Determine the basic problem your product is solving or the primary need it is fulfilling.
2. **Design the MVP**: Develop the simplest version of the product that delivers on this core value.
3. **Launch and Test**: Release the MVP to a segment of your target audience.
4. **Collect and Analyze Feedback**: Gather data on user experiences and preferences.
5. **Iterate**: Refine and improve the product based on feedback and repeat the cycle.

7.6.4 Examples of MVPs

1. **Dropbox**: Dropbox started with a simple video demonstrating its file-syncing solution to test the market's interest, saving time and resources on building the full product.

2. **Airbnb**: Initially, the founders offered their apartment for rent during a conference in their city to validate the demand for a peer-to-peer lodging service.

3. **Zappos**: The founder started by taking pictures of shoes in stores and posting them online to see if people would buy them before setting up a full e-commerce supply chain.

7.6.5 Challenges in Creating an MVP

- **Determining the MVP Features**: Deciding what features are essential for the MVP and what can be left out.
- **Balancing Quality and Simplicity**: Ensuring the MVP is simple but not substandard.
- **Setting and Managing Expectations**: Communicating the purpose of the MVP to stakeholders and managing their expectations.

7.6.6 Best Practices in MVP Development

- **Focus on the Problem**: Ensure the MVP addresses a real problem faced by your target audience.
- **Clear Goals and Metrics**: Set clear objectives for what you want to learn from the MVP and how you will measure success.
- **Iterative Development**: Be prepared to adapt and evolve your MVP based on user feedback.

The Minimum Viable Product is a powerful concept in the realm of innovation and product development. It enables businesses to learn quickly about their market, reduce development costs, and iterate their products based on real user feedback, leading to more successful and user-focused outcomes.

7.7 Prototyping

Prototyping is a crucial step in the design and development process, where ideas are translated into tangible forms. It involves creating an initial model of a product to test and refine concepts before final production. Prototypes range from very basic to highly sophisticated, depending on the stage of the development process and the goals of the prototype.

7.7.1 Purpose of Prototyping

The primary purposes of prototyping include:

- **Concept Validation**: Checking if an idea is feasible.
- **Design Testing**: Identifying design flaws and areas for improvement.
- **User Feedback**: Gathering insights from users to refine the product.
- **Cost Estimation**: Understanding the resources required for production.

7.7.2 Types of Prototypes

1. **Low-Fidelity Prototypes**: Simple, often paper-based models used for quick and early visualization of ideas. They are useful for initial brainstorming and concept discussions.
2. **High-Fidelity Prototypes**: More sophisticated and closer to the final product, used for more accurate testing and user experience assessment.

7.7.3 Prototyping Processes

1. **Idea Sketching**: The initial step where rough ideas are sketched on paper or digitally to explore different concepts.
2. **Mock-ups**: Creating a static model, often using materials like cardboard or foam, to get a sense of size, form, and aesthetics.
3. **Digital Prototypes**: Using software tools to create virtual models, which can be used for more detailed design work and functionality testing.
4. **Physical Prototyping**: Building a working model that users can interact with. This stage often involves 3D printing, CNC machining, or hand-crafting.

7.7.4 Prototyping in Various Industries

- **Product Design**: Creating models of new gadgets, appliances, or tools to test ergonomics, usability, and aesthetics.
- **Software Development**: Developing wireframes and clickable demos for websites or applications to test user interfaces and user experience.
- **Architecture**: Building scale models of buildings or spaces to visualize and refine architectural designs.

7.7.5 Examples of Prototyping

1. **Apple's First iPhone Prototype**: Apple's initial prototype for the iPhone was a large and clunky device, far from the sleek final product. This prototype was essential for testing the core functionalities like touchscreen interface and operating system.
2. **Automotive Industry**: Car manufacturers create full-scale clay models of new vehicles to evaluate design elements visually before finalizing the design for production.
3. **Airbnb's Website Redesign**: Airbnb used prototyping to redesign its website, creating multiple iterations to test features like search functionality and booking processes.

Best Practices in Prototyping

- **Iterate Often**: Continuously refine prototypes based on feedback and testing results.
- **Focus on Key Features**: Concentrate on the most critical aspects of the product to avoid getting bogged down in details.
- **Involve Users Early**: Get feedback from potential users early and often to ensure the product meets their needs and expectations.
- **Balance Fidelity and Speed**: Choose the right level of fidelity for each prototype stage, balancing detail and rapid development.

Prototyping is a vital part of the innovation and development process. It allows designers and developers to explore ideas, test assumptions, and refine products in a cost-effective and risk-reducing manner. Through various types of prototypes, from simple sketches to complex models, prototyping paves the way for creating products that are functional, user-friendly, and market-ready.

7.8 THE PRODUCT LIFECYCLE MODEL

The Product Lifecycle Model is a fundamental concept in marketing and business strategy that describes the stages a product goes through from introduction to market until its eventual decline. Understanding this lifecycle is crucial for managing products effectively over time, optimizing marketing strategies, and maximizing profits.

7.8.1 Stages of the Product Lifecycle

1. **Introduction Stage**: The product is launched into the market. Sales growth is slow due to consumer unfamiliarity. Marketing efforts focus on awareness and early adoption.

2. **Growth Stage**: The product gains acceptance, demand and sales increase rapidly, and profitability improves. Marketing focuses on broader audience targeting.

3. **Maturity Stage**: The product reaches peak market penetration. Sales growth slows as competition increases. Strategies often involve product differentiation and feature enhancements.

4. **Decline Stage**: Sales and profits begin to fall due to market saturation, technological advancements, or changing consumer preferences. Companies may consider product discontinuation or re-innovation.

7.8.2 Applying the Product Lifecycle Model

- **Strategic Planning**: Helps businesses in forecasting, resource allocation, and strategic planning.

- **Marketing Adaptation**: Guides the adaptation of marketing strategies to suit different stages of the product's lifecycle.

- **R&D Focus**: Influences research and development efforts based on the product's stage in the lifecycle.

7.8.3 Examples of the Product Lifecycle Model

1. **The Personal Computer**: In the early 1980s, the personal computer was in its introduction stage with companies like IBM leading the market.

The growth stage saw rapid expansion with players like Apple and Microsoft. It reached maturity in the 2000s, and now, with market saturation and the advent of smartphones, it is in the decline stage for many consumer segments.

2. **Film Cameras**: Film cameras were once at the maturity stage with widespread use. However, the advent of digital cameras pushed them into the decline stage, significantly reducing their market.

7.8.4 Challenges and Considerations
- The length of each stage can vary significantly between products.
- External factors like technological change or competitive actions can abruptly shift the product's lifecycle.
- Not all products follow the standard lifecycle pattern; some may skip or revisit stages.

7.8.5 Best Practices for Managing the Product Lifecycle
- **Continuous Market Research**: To understand changing consumer needs and preferences.
- **Innovation and Adaptation**: Regularly update and innovate the product to stay relevant.
- **Diversification**: Diversify the product portfolio to mitigate risks associated with the lifecycle stages.

The Product Lifecycle Model is an essential framework for understanding the progression of a product in the market. By recognizing and adapting to each stage, businesses can make informed decisions, optimize strategies, and ultimately extend the profitability and relevance of their products.

7.9 LEAD USER METHOD

The Lead User Method, developed by Eric von Hippel, is a revolutionary approach to innovation that involves identifying and collaborating with 'lead users'. These users are individuals or organizations at the forefront of market trends or facing needs that will become common in a market but are unserved by current solutions.

7.9.1 Fundamentals of the Lead User Method
1. **Identifying Lead Users**: They are ahead of market trends and experience needs before the majority of consumers, often driven by a high incentive to solve their problems.
2. **Engaging with Lead Users**: Building relationships with these users to gain deep insights into emerging needs and potential solutions.

7.9.2 Process of the Lead User Method
1. **Laying the Groundwork**: Define the market or domain of interest and the types of innovation sought.
2. **Identifying Trends**: Research to identify emerging trends that are likely to drive market changes.
3. **Finding Lead Users**: Locate individuals or organizations experiencing the needs driven by these trends.
4. **Developing Concepts**: Collaborate with lead users to develop new concepts and solutions.
5. **Prototyping and Testing**: Create prototypes of the new solutions and test them for practicality and marketability.

7.9.3 Advantages of the Lead User Method
- Access to cutting-edge ideas and solutions.
- Early insight into market trends and emerging needs.
- Reduced risk in new product development.
- Potential for breakthrough innovations.

7.9.4 Examples of the Lead User Method
1. **3M's Medical Surgical Masks**: 3M used the Lead User Method to innovate in the field of medical surgical masks. By collaborating with lead users in hospitals, they developed a new mask that significantly reduced the risk of infection.
2. **The Sports Equipment Industry**: Many innovations in sports equipment come from lead users, like extreme athletes, who modify or create new equipment to meet their advanced needs.

7.9.5 Challenges in Implementing the Lead User Method
- Identifying true lead users can be challenging.
- Requires commitment to deep market and user research.
- Collaboration with lead users demands openness to unconventional ideas and solutions.

7.9.6 Best Practices in Applying the Lead User Method
- Engage in thorough and ongoing market trend analysis.
- Foster a corporate culture that values and supports user-led innovation.
- Ensure close and iterative collaboration with lead users throughout the development process.

The Lead User Method is a powerful tool for innovation, particularly useful for companies looking to stay ahead of market trends and create breakthrough products. By focusing on the needs and solutions of lead users, organizations can tap into a source of innovative ideas that have the potential to transform markets.

7.10 A/B TESTING

A/B Testing, also known as split testing, is a method of comparing two versions of a webpage, app, or other digital products to determine which one performs better. It involves showing two variants (A and B) to different segments of users at the same time and comparing which variant drives more conversions or achieves the desired outcome.

7.10.1 Purpose and Importance of A/B Testing
- **Data-Driven Decisions**: A/B testing provides empirical data to make informed decisions about changes or improvements.
- **Optimize User Experience**: It helps in refining the user experience, ensuring that changes lead to positive outcomes.
- **Improve Conversion Rates**: By testing different elements, businesses can identify what works best for converting visitors into customers.

7.10.2 Elements Often Tested in A/B Testing
1. **Call-to-Action Buttons**: Their size, color, and wording.

2. **Page Layouts**: The arrangement of text, images, and other elements.
3. **Content and Headlines**: Variations in language, tone, and style.
4. **Navigation Paths**: Different ways users can navigate through a site or app.
5. **Features and Functionalities**: Testing new features against the status quo.

7.10.3 Process of Conducting A/B Testing

- **Identify Goal**: Clearly define what you are trying to achieve (e.g., increase click-through rate).
- **Create Variants**: Develop two versions of the product where one element is varied.
- **Run the Test**: Randomly assign users to each version and let them interact.
- **Collect Data**: Gather data on user interactions and conversions.
- **Analyze Results**: Use statistical methods to determine which version performed better.

7.10.4 Examples of A/B Testing

1. **E-commerce Websites**: Testing different layouts of a product page to see which results in more sales.
2. **Email Marketing Campaigns**: Sending two different email versions to see which has a higher open or click rate.
3. **Social Media Ads**: Running two ad variants to determine which garners more engagement or leads.

7.10.5 Challenges in A/B Testing

- Ensuring a statistically significant sample size to make reliable conclusions.
- Avoiding biased or skewed results due to external factors like holidays or special events.

- Interpreting results correctly and understanding that what works for one audience may not work for another.

7.10.6 Best Practices for Effective A/B Testing
- **Test One Change at a Time**: To clearly understand which element affects performance.
- **Ensure Statistical Significance**: Enough data must be collected to make valid conclusions.
- **Consider External Factors**: Be aware of external influences that could affect the results.
- **Repeat Tests**: Run tests multiple times to verify results.

A/B testing is a powerful tool for optimizing digital products, offering insights into user preferences and behavior. It helps in making precise, data-driven decisions, enhancing the user experience, and ultimately driving better business outcomes.

7.11 Stress Test

A stress test, in the context of innovation and business, is a method used to evaluate how a product, service, or system functions under extreme or unexpected conditions. It is designed to push the boundaries of normal operation to identify potential weaknesses and areas for improvement.

7.11.1 Purpose and Importance of Stress Testing
- **Identifying Vulnerabilities**: Stress tests reveal potential failure points in a product or system that might not be visible under normal conditions.
- **Ensuring Reliability**: By understanding and addressing these vulnerabilities, companies can ensure greater reliability and performance.
- **Building Customer Trust**: Products that withstand stress tests are more likely to gain and retain customer trust.

7.11.2 Types of Stress Tests
1. **Physical Stress Test**: For tangible products, this involves testing beyond the usual physical limits like excess weight, pressure, or temperature.

2. **Digital Stress Test**: For software and digital services, this means testing the system's capacity to handle high traffic, data loads, or security threats.

3. **Environmental Stress Test**: Evaluating a product's durability in various environmental conditions like humidity, altitude, or corrosive environments.

7.11.3 Process of Conducting a Stress Test

- **Planning and Goal Setting**: Define what aspects of the product or service are being tested and what thresholds or conditions will be used.

- **Execution**: Carry out the test by subjecting the product or service to the defined stress conditions.

- **Monitoring and Data Collection**: Carefully monitor the process and collect relevant data on how the product or system performs.

- **Analysis and Improvement**: Analyze the results to identify weaknesses and implement improvements.

7.11.4 Examples of Stress Testing

1. **Smartphone Durability Tests**: Smartphone manufacturers often conduct stress tests like drop tests, water resistance tests, and bend tests to ensure durability.

2. **Website Crash Tests**: Companies with high-traffic websites, like online retailers, often conduct stress tests to see how much user traffic the site can handle before crashing or slowing down significantly.

3. **Aircraft Testing**: Aircraft are subjected to extreme stress tests including wing flex tests and emergency system tests to ensure safety and functionality under extreme conditions.

7.11.5 Challenges in Stress Testing

- Determining realistic yet challenging test conditions.

- Balancing the cost and time of conducting comprehensive stress tests.

- Interpreting data accurately to make meaningful improvements.

7.11.6 Best Practices for Effective Stress Testing
- **Comprehensive Planning**: Ensure that the stress test covers a broad range of potential scenarios.
- **Realistic Simulation**: Create conditions that closely mimic potential real-world extremes.
- **Iterative Approach**: Use the results from initial tests to refine and conduct subsequent tests for continuous improvement.

Stress testing is an essential component of product development and quality assurance. It ensures that products and services can withstand extreme conditions, thereby safeguarding the company's reputation and customer satisfaction. By rigorously applying stress tests, businesses can preemptively address potential issues, leading to stronger, more reliable offerings.

7.12 THE ADOPTION CURVE

The Adoption Curve, also known as the Diffusion of Innovations Theory, was popularized by Everett Rogers in 1962. It's a model that seeks to explain how, why, and at what rate new ideas and technology spread. The Adoption Curve categorizes consumers into different groups based on their willingness to adopt a new product or innovation.

7.12.1 The Five Stages of the Adoption Curve
1. **Innovators (2.5%)**: These are the first individuals to adopt an innovation. They are risk-takers and are willing to try new ideas at a potential loss.
2. **Early Adopters (13.5%)**: This group represents opinion leaders. They adopt new ideas early but carefully and help spread word-of-mouth.
3. **Early Majority (34%)**: They are rarely leaders, but they do adopt new ideas before the average person. This group typically requires seeing evidence that the innovation works before investing.
4. **Late Majority (34%)**: They are skeptical of change and will only adopt an innovation after it has been tried by the majority.
5. **Laggards (16%)**: The last to adopt an innovation. They are bound by tradition and very conservative.

7.12.2 Significance of the Adoption Curve in Business

Understanding where your product lies on the Adoption Curve is crucial for developing effective marketing strategies and product development. Tailoring your approach to each segment can significantly enhance the adoption rate.

7.12.3 Examples of the Adoption Curve

1. **Smartphones**: Initially adopted by innovators and early adopters, who were tech-savvy and saw the potential of having a powerful device in their pocket. Over time, as smartphones became more user-friendly and practical, the early and late majority started adopting them, making them ubiquitous.

2. **Electric Cars**: Electric vehicles first appealed to innovators and early adopters who were interested in technology and environmental sustainability. Only recently are they beginning to move into the early majority phase, as infrastructure improves and prices become more accessible.

7.12.4 Challenges in Navigating the Adoption Curve

- Understanding the unique needs and motivations of each group.

- Developing appropriate marketing and communication strategies for different stages.

- Managing the innovation's lifecycle to maintain relevance and appeal.

7.12.5 Strategies for Success

- **Targeted Marketing**: Develop and adjust marketing strategies to appeal to each segment of the adoption curve.

- **Continuous Innovation**: Keep improving the product to appeal to later adopters.

- **Feedback Loop**: Use feedback from early adopters to refine and improve the product for subsequent segments.

The Adoption Curve is a powerful tool for understanding how innovations spread through different segments of the market. By recognizing the characteristics and needs of each group, businesses can strategically guide their products through these stages, maximizing adoption and success in the market.

7.13 THE CHASM

'The Chasm' is a concept popularized by Geoffrey A. Moore in his book "Crossing the Chasm." It refers to a critical gap between the early adopters of a product and the early majority in the technology adoption lifecycle. This concept is crucial for understanding why some innovations achieve mainstream success while others falter.

7.13.1 Understanding the Technology Adoption Lifecycle

Before delving into the Chasm, it's essential to understand the five segments of the Technology Adoption Lifecycle:

1. **Innovators**: Those who are first to try new technology.
2. **Early Adopters**: Visionaries who see the potential value of the innovation.
3. **Early Majority**: Pragmatists who adopt new technology when its practicality is proven.
4. **Late Majority**: Conservatives who are skeptical of change and adopt technology late.
5. **Laggards**: The last to adopt, often resistant to change.

7.13.2 The Chasm: Between Early Adopters and Early Majority

The Chasm lies between the Early Adopters and the Early Majority. While early adopters are willing to overlook imperfections for the sake of innovation, the early majority needs reliable, effective solutions. This shift in expectations creates a gap – the Chasm – which can be fatal for a new product if not navigated carefully.

7.13.3 Crossing the Chasm

Crossing the Chasm requires strategic shifts:

- **Focus on Market Niches**: Target specific niches within the early majority, tailoring the product to their specific needs.
- **Enhance Product Reliability and Usability**: Ensure the product is user-friendly and reliable to appeal to the pragmatic early majority.

- **Develop Effective Marketing Strategies**: Shift from visionary appeal to focusing on practicality and usability.

7.13.4 Examples of Crossing the Chasm

1. **Smartphones**: Initially, smartphones were used by technophiles and innovators. Companies like Apple successfully crossed the Chasm by making smartphones user-friendly and practical for the early majority, leading to widespread adoption.

2. **Electric Cars**: Electric vehicles initially appealed primarily to environmental visionaries. Companies like Tesla are working to cross the Chasm by improving the practical aspects like range, charging infrastructure, and cost.

7.13.5 Challenges in Crossing the Chasm

- Misunderstanding the market needs of the early majority.
- Underestimating the importance of product reliability and support.
- Failing to adapt marketing strategies for a more pragmatic audience.

7.13.6 Strategies for Success

- **In-depth Market Research**: Understand the specific needs and concerns of the early majority.
- **Strong Customer Support**: Provide robust support and service to build trust.
- **Strategic Alliances and Partnerships**: Collaborate with established players to gain credibility and access to broader markets.

The Chasm is a critical phase in the technology adoption lifecycle that determines whether an innovation will make the leap to broader market acceptance. Successfully navigating this phase requires understanding the distinct needs of different market segments and strategically adapting product development and marketing approaches.

7.14 Net Promoter Score (NPS)

The Net Promoter Score (NPS) is a widely used market research metric that gauges customer loyalty and satisfaction with a company or product. Developed by Fred Reichheld, Bain & Company, and Satmetrix in 2003, NPS is based on a single survey question that asks customers to rate the likelihood that they would recommend a company, product, or service to friends or colleagues.

7.14.1 Understanding NPS

NPS is calculated based on responses to the question: "On a scale of 0 to 10, how likely are you to recommend our company/product/service to a friend or colleague?" Respondents are grouped into three categories:

1. **Promoters (score 9-10)**: Loyal customers who will keep buying and refer others, fueling growth.
2. **Passives (score 7-8)**: Satisfied but unenthusiastic customers, vulnerable to competitive offerings.
3. **Detractors (score 0-6)**: Unhappy customers who can damage the brand and impede growth through negative word-of-mouth.

7.14.2 Calculating NPS

NPS is calculated by subtracting the percentage of Detractors from the percentage of Promoters. The score can range from -100 (if every customer is a Detractor) to 100 (if every customer is a Promoter).

7.14.3 Importance of NPS

- **Measure of Customer Loyalty**: NPS provides a straightforward metric to track customer loyalty and satisfaction.
- **Predictor of Business Growth**: A high NPS is often correlated with repeat business and referrals.
- **Feedback for Improvement**: NPS can highlight areas needing improvement and can help in making strategic decisions.

7.14.4 Examples of NPS Usage

1. **Service Industries**: Hotels and airlines use NPS to gauge customer satisfaction and predict the likelihood of repeat patronage.
2. **Retail**: Retail companies measure NPS to understand customer loyalty and the effectiveness of their customer service.
3. **SaaS Companies**: Software companies use NPS to assess user satisfaction with their products, often correlating it with renewal rates.

7.14.5 Challenges and Criticisms of NPS
- Oversimplification: Some argue that NPS oversimplifies customer sentiment into just three categories.
- Cultural Bias: The way people respond to surveys can vary significantly across different cultures.
- Lack of Context: NPS does not provide detailed insights into why customers are promoters or detractors.

7.14.6 Best Practices for Using NPS
- **Regular Measurement**: Regularly track NPS to observe trends and measure the impact of changes.
- **Combine with Qualitative Data**: Use follow-up questions to understand the reasons behind the scores.
- **Act on Feedback**: Use NPS data to make informed decisions to improve customer experience.

Net Promoter Score is a valuable tool for measuring customer loyalty and predicting business growth. While it should not be the sole metric for customer satisfaction, when used correctly and in combination with other qualitative insights, NPS can provide powerful guidance for business strategy and customer relationship management.

7.15 GARTNER MAGIC QUADRANT
The Gartner Magic Quadrant is a research methodology and graphical representation used by Gartner, a leading IT research and advisory company, to evaluate technology providers within a specific market. It's a valuable tool for stakeholders looking to understand the positioning of technology players in a competitive landscape.

7.15.1 Components of the Gartner Magic Quadrant
The Magic Quadrant is divided into four types of technology providers:

1. **Leaders**: Demonstrate a strong ability to execute and a completeness of vision. They are well-established market players who are often the benchmark for other competitors.

2. **Challengers**: Have a strong ability to execute but may lack a complete vision. They are typically strong performers with robust capabilities but may not be as innovative.
3. **Visionaries**: Have a strong understanding of where the market is headed (completeness of vision) but may struggle with execution. They are often innovators and disruptors.
4. **Niche Players**: Focus on a small segment of the market or a specialized offering. They may excel in their specific area but struggle to expand their reach or impact.

7.15.2 Purpose and Importance of the Magic Quadrant

- **Market Insight**: Provides insights into the direction, maturity, and participants in a market.
- **Vendor Comparison**: Helps businesses compare technology providers in terms of their strengths and weaknesses.
- **Strategic Decision-Making**: Assists in making informed decisions about technology investments and partnerships.

7.15.3 Methodology Behind the Magic Quadrant

- **Data Collection**: Gartner analysts conduct rigorous research, including vendor briefings, client interviews, and analysis of financial and market performance.
- **Evaluation Criteria**: Vendors are evaluated on two primary dimensions: 'Ability to Execute' and 'Completeness of Vision'.
- **Continuous Update**: The Quadrant is updated regularly to reflect changing market dynamics.

7.15.4 Examples of Gartner Magic Quadrant Usage

1. **Cloud Services**: Businesses use the Magic Quadrant to evaluate and select cloud service providers, comparing giants like AWS, Microsoft Azure, and Google Cloud.
2. **Enterprise Resource Planning (ERP) Systems**: Companies consult the Quadrant to choose an ERP system, evaluating vendors like SAP, Oracle, and Microsoft.

7.15.5 Challenges and Criticisms

- **Subjectivity**: Some argue that the Magic Quadrant can be subjective, as it relies on the judgment of Gartner's analysts.

- **Broad Categorization**: The broad categories may oversimplify the strengths and weaknesses of vendors.

- **Dynamic Markets**: Rapidly changing technology markets may mean that the Quadrant doesn't always reflect the most current state of the market.

7.15.6 Best Practices for Interpreting the Magic Quadrant

- **Contextual Understanding**: Use the Quadrant as a starting point, not the sole basis for decision-making.

- **Complementary Research**: Supplement the Quadrant with additional research and due diligence.

- **Industry Specificity**: Consider the specific needs and context of your industry when interpreting the Quadrant.

The Gartner Magic Quadrant is a valuable tool for businesses looking to navigate the complex landscape of technology providers. While it should be used as part of a broader decision-making process, it offers a useful framework for assessing market leaders, challengers, visionaries, and niche players.

7.16 THE ANSOFF MATRIX

The Ansoff Matrix, created by Igor Ansoff in 1957, is a strategic planning tool that provides a framework to help executives, senior managers, and marketers devise strategies for future growth. The matrix presents four strategies for growth by varying products and markets.

7.16.1 The Four Strategies of the Ansoff Matrix

1. **Market Penetration**: Focuses on increasing sales of *existing products* to the *existing market*. This involves strategies like price promotions, increased marketing, and competitive tactics.

2. **Product Development**: Involves developing *new products* for the *existing market*. This strategy leverages customer loyalty and brand strength to introduce and sell new products.

3. **Market Development**: Entails entering *new markets* with *existing products*. This might include expanding into new geographical areas or targeting new customer segments.

4. **Diversification**: The most risky strategy, involving introducing *new products* to *new markets*. This could be related diversification (products are somewhat related to existing ones) or unrelated diversification (completely new products and markets).

7.16.2 Importance of the Ansoff Matrix

- **Strategic Clarity**: Helps in clearly identifying the direction for growth strategies.
- **Risk Management**: Assesses different levels of risk associated with various growth strategies.
- **Resource Allocation**: Aids in decision-making about where to allocate resources for maximum impact.

7.16.3 Application of the Ansoff Matrix in Business

- Companies use the matrix to plan and implement growth strategies based on their market position and product portfolio.
- It provides a structured approach to evaluate the potential and risk of different growth strategies.

7.16.4 Examples of the Ansoff Matrix in Action

1. **Apple's Product Development**: Apple frequently employs the product development strategy by introducing innovative products like the iPhone, iPad, and Apple Watch to its existing market.

2. **Starbucks' Market Development**: Starbucks' expansion into international markets like China and India is an example of market development.

3. **Google's Diversification**: Google has diversified into new markets and products with ventures like Google Cloud, Waymo (self-driving cars), and more, moving beyond its core search engine business.

7.16.5 Challenges in Applying the Ansoff Matrix
- **Market Uncertainty**: Especially in diversification and market development, predicting market behavior can be challenging.
- **Resource Constraints**: Adequate resources are required to execute strategies, particularly in diversification.
- **Balancing Risk and Reward**: Higher growth strategies come with increased risk, and balancing this can be complex.

7.16.6 Best Practices for Using the Ansoff Matrix
- **Comprehensive Market Research**: Understanding market dynamics and customer needs.
- **Assessment of Capabilities**: Evaluating whether the organization has the necessary resources and competencies.
- **Continuous Review and Adaptation**: Regularly reviewing strategies in light of changing market conditions and organizational objectives.

The Ansoff Matrix remains a valuable tool for strategic planning, offering a clear framework for understanding the different avenues for growth. By considering the various risks and potentials of each quadrant, businesses can make more informed decisions about their growth strategies.

7.17 THE MCKINSEY MATRIX
The McKinsey Matrix, also known as the GE-McKinsey Nine-Box Matrix, is a strategic tool used for analyzing a company's business portfolio and making decisions about where to prioritize resources. Developed in the 1970s by McKinsey & Company for General Electric, the matrix helps businesses evaluate their business units in terms of their market attractiveness and competitive strength.

7.17.1 Understanding the McKinsey Matrix
The matrix is a 3x3 grid with the following dimensions:

- **Vertical Axis (Market Attractiveness)**: Factors like market growth, market size, and profit margins define how attractive a market is.
- **Horizontal Axis (Competitive Strength)**: This includes aspects like market share, product quality, and brand strength.

The grid is divided into nine cells, each representing a different strategic decision area ranging from 'invest and grow' to 'harvest or divest'.

7.17.2 Using the McKinsey Matrix for Strategic Analysis
- **Classification of Business Units**: Place each business unit in one of the nine cells based on its market attractiveness and competitive strength.
- **Strategic Decision Making**: Use the positioning to decide where to focus, invest, grow, or divest.

7.17.3 Examples of the McKinsey Matrix Application
1. **Diversified Corporations**: Large corporations with multiple business units use the McKinsey Matrix to allocate resources effectively across units.
2. **Investment Firms**: Investment companies may use the matrix to assess which industries or companies present the best opportunity for investment.

7.17.4 Benefits of the McKinsey Matrix
- Provides a clear and straightforward framework for portfolio analysis.
- Helps in allocating resources in a balanced manner across different business units.
- Assists in strategic thinking about the growth potential and competitive position of each unit.

7.17.5 Challenges in Implementing the McKinsey Matrix
- **Subjectivity**: The assessment of market attractiveness and competitive strength can be subjective.
- **Dynamic Markets**: Rapid changes in the market can quickly render an analysis outdated.
- **Over-Simplification**: Some critics argue that the matrix may oversimplify complex strategic decisions.

7.17.6 Best Practices for Using the McKinsey Matrix
- **Comprehensive Market Research**: To accurately assess market attractiveness.

- **Objective Evaluation**: Aim for objectivity in assessing competitive strength.
- **Regular Updates**: Update the matrix regularly to reflect changing market conditions.

The McKinsey Matrix is a valuable tool for businesses with diverse portfolios, providing a structured approach to analyzing and prioritizing investments in different business units. By assessing both market attractiveness and competitive strength, companies can make more informed strategic decisions about where to allocate resources.

7.18 The BCG Matrix

The Boston Consulting Group (BCG) Matrix, developed in the 1970s by Bruce Henderson, is a strategic tool used for portfolio analysis in business management and marketing. It helps companies evaluate their product lines or business units in terms of market growth and market share.

7.18.1 Understanding the BCG Matrix

The matrix is divided into four quadrants based on two dimensions: market growth and market share. Each quadrant represents a different type of product or business unit:

1. **Stars**: High market growth, high market share. These are leaders in a growing market.
2. **Question Marks (or Problem Children)**: High market growth, low market share. These have potential but need investment to grow.
3. **Cash Cows**: Low market growth, high market share. Mature, successful products with little need for investment.
4. **Dogs**: Low market growth, low market share. These are least profitable or may even be loss-makers.

7.18.2 Purpose and Importance of the BCG Matrix

- **Strategic Decision Making**: Assists in making decisions about which products or business units to invest in, develop, or divest.
- **Resource Allocation**: Helps in allocating resources effectively among different business units or product lines.

- **Portfolio Analysis**: Provides a simple visual representation of a company's product or business portfolio.

7.18.3 Application of the BCG Matrix in Business
- Businesses use the BCG Matrix to categorize and evaluate different segments of their product portfolio, aligning investment and strategic focus accordingly.

7.18.4 Examples of the BCG Matrix Application
1. **Apple Inc.**: Apple's iPhone line could be considered a 'Star', commanding high market share in a growing market, whereas some of its older iPod products might fall into the 'Dog' category.
2. **Automotive Companies**: A car manufacturer may classify its electric vehicles as 'Question Marks' due to their potential for growth in a rapidly evolving market.

7.18.5 Challenges and Limitations of the BCG Matrix
- **Oversimplification**: The matrix may oversimplify complex market dynamics and competitive factors.
- **Static Analysis**: It provides a snapshot in time and doesn't account for market dynamics.
- **Subjective Classification**: Determining the exact position of a product or business unit can be subjective and may vary based on the criteria used.

7.18.6 Best Practices for Using the BCG Matrix
- **Dynamic Review**: Regularly update the matrix to reflect changes in the market and business.
- **Integrated Approach**: Use the BCG Matrix as part of a broader strategic analysis toolkit.
- **Market and Competitive Analysis**: Complement the matrix with in-depth market and competitive analyses.

The BCG Matrix is a valuable tool for strategic portfolio management, offering a straightforward way to evaluate product lines and business units in terms of their market performance and potential. While it should not be used in isolation, it provides essential insights for effective decision-making in resource allocation and strategy development.

7.19 Innovation Roadmap

An innovation roadmap is a strategic planning tool that outlines the steps needed to move from current operations and products to a future with innovative changes. It combines the elements of business strategy with the dynamic process of innovation, providing a structured visual representation of the innovation journey.

7.19.1 Purpose and Importance of an Innovation Roadmap

- **Guiding Strategic Innovations**: Helps in systematically planning and guiding the process of innovation within an organization.

- **Resource Allocation**: Assists in determining where and how to allocate resources for innovation.

- **Stakeholder Alignment**: Ensures that all stakeholders are aligned and understand the innovation objectives and the steps needed to achieve them.

7.19.2 Components of an Innovation Roadmap

1. **Strategic Objectives**: Clear definition of what the organization aims to achieve through innovation.

2. **Innovation Initiatives**: Specific projects or initiatives that will drive the innovation process.

3. **Timeline**: A timeline for the implementation of innovation initiatives, including key milestones.

4. **Resources**: Identification of the resources required for each initiative, including budget, personnel, and technology.

5. **Risk Assessment**: An evaluation of potential risks and obstacles and strategies to mitigate them.

7.19.3 Developing an Innovation Roadmap

- **Understand the Current State**: Assess the current products, processes, and market position.

- **Define Innovation Goals**: Clearly state what the organization seeks to achieve through innovation.
- **Identify Key Initiatives**: Determine the projects or changes that will lead to innovation.
- **Plan the Roadmap**: Outline the timeline, resource allocation, and responsibilities.
- **Implement and Review**: Execute the roadmap and regularly review progress, adapting as necessary.

7.19.4 Examples of Innovation Roadmaps

1. **Technology Company**: A tech company might have a roadmap for developing a new suite of AI-powered tools, detailing research, development, testing, and market launch phases.
2. **Manufacturing Firm**: A roadmap for implementing automation and IoT within production processes, including pilot projects, full-scale implementation, and training programs.

7.19.5 Challenges in Creating an Innovation Roadmap

- **Uncertainty and Change**: Innovation is inherently uncertain, making it difficult to predict outcomes and timelines accurately.
- **Resource Constraints**: Adequate funding, skilled personnel, and technology may be limited.
- **Stakeholder Buy-in**: Ensuring all stakeholders, from leadership to employees, support and understand the roadmap.

7.19.6 Best Practices for an Effective Innovation Roadmap

- **Flexibility**: Allow for adjustments as new information and opportunities emerge.
- **Collaboration**: Involve different departments and stakeholders in creating the roadmap.
- **Clear Communication**: Regularly communicate progress, changes, and results to all relevant parties.

- **Metrics and Monitoring**: Establish metrics to measure progress and impact of innovation initiatives.

An innovation roadmap is a vital tool for any organization looking to navigate the complex journey of innovation. It offers a clear, structured path from the current state to a future of growth and innovation, aligning resources, activities, and stakeholders towards common innovation goals.

7.20 THE 4 U OF PROBLEMS WORTH SOLVING

The 4 U framework is a strategic tool used to identify and assess problems worth solving in the business and innovation landscape. It comprises four key aspects: Unworkable, Unavoidable, Urgent, and Underserved. This framework helps innovators and entrepreneurs focus on issues that are critical and likely to yield significant value when addressed.

7.20.1 Understanding the 4 U Framework

1. **Unavoidable**: These are problems that are inevitable and cannot be avoided. For example, complying with new regulations or laws.

2. **Urgent**: These are problems that require immediate attention and resolution. For example, a medical emergency or a security breach.

3. **Unworkable**: These are problems where existing solutions are not practical or effective. For example, outdated technology or inefficient processes.

4. **Underserved**: These are problems that lack adequate solutions or are not being addressed by existing solutions. For example, niche markets or unmet needs.

7.20.2 Application of the 4 U Framework

- **Prioritizing Innovation Efforts**: Use the framework to identify areas that are most in need of innovative solutions and prioritize efforts accordingly.

- **Assessing Market Potential**: Evaluate whether a problem, and its potential solution, has enough market demand to be viable.

- **Guiding Product Development**: Focus product development on addressing these key problem areas.

7.20.3 Examples of the 4 U Framework in Action

5. **Unworkable**: The complexity of tax filing systems creates an unworkable problem for individuals and businesses, leading to solutions like automated tax preparation software.

6. **Unavoidable**: Healthcare compliance in hospitals is unavoidable, and innovations in compliance management software can significantly aid in this area.

7. **Urgent**: Cybersecurity threats pose an urgent problem for businesses and individuals, necessitating immediate and effective security solutions.

8. **Underserved**: In many rural areas, access to quality healthcare is underserved, presenting opportunities for telemedicine and mobile health clinics.

7.20.4 Challenges in Applying the 4 U Framework

- **Identifying Real Problems**: Distinguishing between superficial issues and deep-rooted problems that fit the 4 U criteria.

- **Market Viability**: Ensuring that the solution to these problems is economically viable and sustainable.

- **Balancing Resource Allocation**: Effectively allocating resources to address these problems without overextending.

7.20.5 Best Practices for Using the 4 U Framework

- **Comprehensive Research**: Conduct in-depth market and user research to identify and understand the problems.

- **Stakeholder Engagement**: Engage with potential users and other stakeholders to validate the problems and understand their needs.

- **Iterative Development**: Develop solutions iteratively, incorporating feedback to ensure that the problem is being effectively addressed.

The 4 U framework provides a valuable lens for identifying and assessing problems that are worth solving. By focusing on issues that are unworkable, unavoidable, urgent, and underserved, innovators and businesses can create solutions that not only meet market needs but also have the potential to make a significant impact.

7.21 The Eisenhower Matrix for Innovation Management

The Eisenhower Matrix, also known as the Urgent-Important Matrix, is a time management tool that helps prioritize tasks based on their urgency and importance. While traditionally used for personal productivity, this matrix can be effectively adapted for innovation management, enabling organizations to prioritize innovation initiatives effectively.

The Eisenhower Matrix in Innovation Management

The matrix divides tasks into four quadrants:

1. **Quadrant I - Urgent and Important**: Tasks that require immediate attention and are critical for innovation success. These often involve resolving issues that could hinder ongoing innovation projects.

2. **Quadrant II - Not Urgent but Important**: Long-term innovation strategies and development that are important for future success but do not require immediate action.

3. **Quadrant III - Urgent but Not Important**: Day-to-day activities that are urgent but do not significantly contribute to the overall innovation goals.

4. **Quadrant IV - Neither Urgent nor Important**: Low-priority tasks that offer little to no value in achieving innovation objectives.

7.21.1 Purpose and Importance in Innovation Management

- **Strategic Prioritization**: Helps innovation leaders focus on activities that are most beneficial for the organization's innovation goals.

- **Resource Allocation**: Aids in allocating resources, including time and budget, more effectively.

- **Avoiding Overload**: Prevents innovation teams from becoming overwhelmed with non-critical tasks.

7.21.2 Application in Organizational Context
- **Innovation Project Assessment**: Evaluate and categorize ongoing and proposed innovation projects into the four quadrants.
- **Decision Making**: Use the matrix as a guide to make strategic decisions about which projects to pursue, delay, or abandon.

7.21.3 Examples of the Eisenhower Matrix in Innovation Context
1. **Quadrant I - Critical R&D Project**: An urgent and important project to develop a new product that addresses a recently identified market need.
2. **Quadrant II - Future Technology Exploration**: Research into emerging technologies that could impact the industry in the long term, like AI or blockchain.
3. **Quadrant III - Regular Team Meetings**: Routine meetings that are necessary but might not significantly impact the innovation outcome.
4. **Quadrant IV - Outdated Practices**: Continuing legacy practices that no longer add value to current innovation processes.

7.21.4 Challenges in Using the Eisenhower Matrix for Innovation
- **Subjective Categorization**: Determining what is urgent or important can be subjective and vary between individuals.
- **Dynamic Nature of Innovation**: The urgency and importance of tasks can quickly change in response to market or technological developments.
- **Balancing Quadrants**: Ensuring that sufficient attention is given to Quadrant II, which is crucial for long-term innovation success.

7.21.5 Best Practices for Implementing the Matrix
- **Regular Review**: Regularly reassess tasks and projects as priorities and business environments change.
- **Team Alignment**: Ensure that the whole innovation team understands and agrees on the prioritization.
- **Complement with Other Tools**: Use the matrix alongside other innovation management tools for comprehensive planning and analysis.

Adapting the Eisenhower Matrix for innovation management offers a simple yet effective approach to prioritizing tasks and projects. It enables innovation leaders to focus on what truly matters, ensuring that both immediate and long-term innovation goals are met.

7.22 Project Triage

Project Triage is a crucial process in project management, akin to its medical counterpart, where projects or tasks are prioritized based on urgency, importance, and resource availability. This process is essential in ensuring that critical projects are delivered efficiently, especially in environments with multiple competing priorities.

7.22.1 Understanding Project Triage

- **Prioritization**: Assigning levels of importance and urgency to different projects.

- **Resource Allocation**: Allocating resources based on the triage results to ensure optimal use.

- **Agility**: Ability to quickly adapt and re-prioritize as project dynamics change.

7.22.2 The Process of Project Triage

1. **Assessment**: Evaluate all ongoing and planned projects based on factors like deadlines, impact, resources required, and strategic value.

2. **Categorization**: Classify projects into categories such as high priority (immediate action needed), medium priority (necessary but not urgent), and low priority (can be delayed or reconsidered).

3. **Decision Making**: Decide on the course of action for each project – proceed, pause, re-scope, or cancel.

7.22.3 Examples of Project Triage

1. **Software Development**: Prioritizing bug fixes and feature development based on user impact and development capacity.

2. **Event Management**: Deciding which aspects of an event (like venue booking, marketing, guest invitations) need immediate attention based on timelines and impact.

7.22.4 Challenges in Implementing Project Triage
- **Subjectivity in Prioritization**: Balancing differing views on what is urgent or important.
- **Resource Constraints**: Limited resources might make it challenging to address all high-priority projects.
- **Dynamic Project Environments**: Constant changes in project environments can complicate the triage process.

7.22.5 Best Practices for Effective Project Triage
- **Regular Review Meetings**: Conduct frequent meetings to reassess priorities and reallocate resources.
- **Transparent Communication**: Clearly communicate the reasoning behind prioritization decisions to all stakeholders.
- **Flexibility**: Be prepared to adjust priorities as new information or situations arise.

Project Triage is a vital process in project management, enabling organizations to navigate complex environments by systematically assessing, categorizing, and prioritizing projects. Implementing effective project triage ensures that resources are optimally used and critical projects are delivered successfully.

7.23 Transaction Cost Economics in the Context of Innovation

Transaction Cost Economics (TCE) is a theory primarily associated with the work of economist Ronald Coase and later developed by Oliver Williamson. It focuses on the costs incurred in making an economic exchange. When applied to innovation, TCE helps in understanding the decision-making process regarding whether to create innovative solutions in-house or outsource them.

7.23.1 Core Concepts of Transaction Cost Economics
1. **Transaction Costs**: These are the costs related to making an economic exchange. They include search and information costs, bargaining costs, and policing and enforcement costs.
2. **Contracting**: Decision-making between creating (in-house development) or buying (outsourcing) based on which approach is more cost-effective.

3. **Opportunism and Bounded Rationality**: Innovators must consider the risk of opportunism by partners and acknowledge their own bounded rationality (limited by the amount of information they can process) in decision-making.

7.23.2 TCE in the Innovation Process
- **Make or Buy Decisions**: Firms use TCE to decide whether to develop new technologies internally or outsource innovation to external entities.
- **Managing Innovation Partnerships**: TCE helps in understanding and managing the costs and risks associated with partnerships, joint ventures, or alliances for innovation.

7.23.3 Examples in Innovation Context
1. **R&D in Pharmaceutical Companies**: Pharma companies often weigh the costs of conducting R&D in-house versus partnering with biotech firms or universities.
2. **Technology Startups and Outsourcing**: Many startups face decisions about developing technology solutions internally versus outsourcing to specialized firms to reduce costs and focus on core competencies.

7.23.4 Transaction Costs in Innovation
- **Search and Information Costs**: Finding potential partners or evaluating the feasibility of an innovative project.
- **Bargaining Costs**: Negotiating terms and conditions with partners or suppliers.
- **Policing and Enforcement Costs**: Ensuring that all parties adhere to agreements, especially in joint ventures or collaborations.

7.23.5 Challenges in Applying TCE to Innovation
- **Measuring Costs**: Quantifying certain transaction costs can be challenging.
- **Dynamic Nature of Innovation**: The innovation landscape is dynamic, and transaction costs can change rapidly.
- **Intellectual Property Concerns**: In innovation, concerns over IP rights can significantly impact transaction costs.

7.23.6 Best Practices for Applying TCE in Innovation Management

- **Comprehensive Cost Analysis**: Consider all forms of transaction costs, not just financial ones.

- **Flexibility in Contracts**: Create flexible contracts to accommodate the dynamic nature of innovative projects.

- **Risk Management**: Develop strategies to manage the risks associated with opportunism and bounded rationality.

Transaction Cost Economics provides a valuable framework for decision-making in the innovation process, particularly in the make-or-buy decisions. Understanding and effectively managing transaction costs can lead to more efficient and cost-effective innovation strategies, allowing firms to allocate their resources more judiciously in the pursuit of innovation.

7.24 THE INSTRUMENT SELECTION FRAMEWORK

The Instrument Selection Framework (ISF), as developed by Dirk Ploss, Senior Innovation Manager at Beiersdorf, is a strategic tool designed to simplify decision-making in innovation management. This framework assists in determining the most suitable among the 12 major innovation instruments for a specific project. These instruments include:

1. **Basic Research/Applied Sciences**: Focuses on fundamental scientific research.

2. **Innovation Labs**: Dedicated spaces for developing new ideas and technologies.

3. **Open Innovation**: Collaborating with external entities for innovation.

4. **Corporate Venture Capital (CVC)**: Investing in external startups to drive innovation.

5. **Product Development**: Developing new products or improving existing ones.

6. **Incubators**: Supporting early-stage startups to develop their ideas.

7. **Company Building**: Creating new businesses within an organization.

8. **Accelerators**: Fast-tracking startup development.

9. **Intrapreneurship Programs**: Encouraging employees to develop new business ideas.

10. **Task Forces**: Temporary groups focused on specific innovation projects.

11. **Venture Clienting**: Partnering with startups to solve specific business problems.

12. **Mergers & Acquisitions (M&A)**: Acquiring or merging with other companies for innovation growth.

The ISF aids in choosing these instruments by considering factors like time horizon (short, mid, or long-term) and approach (inside-out vs. outside-in). For instance, basic research and innovation labs have a long-term, inside-out focus, whereas intrapreneurship programs and M&A are short-term, with the former being inside-out and the latter outside-in.

This framework can help businesses make specific and best decisions depending on different situations. It's simple and binary but leaves room to move: you always must adapt what comes out of it to your company's needs.

INSIDE-OUT									OUTSIDE-IN								
Long-term			Medium-term			Short-term			Long-term			Medium-term			Short-term		
CORE	EDGE	NEW	CORE	EDGE	NEW	CORE	EDGE	NEW	CORE	EDGE	NEW	CORE	EDGE	NEW	CORE	EDGE	NEW
Basic Research/ Applied Research	Innovation Lab	Intrapreneurship Program	Product Development	Incubation	Incubation/ Intrapreneurship Program	Task Force	Intrapreneurship Program	Intrapreneurship Program	Open Innovation	Corporate Venture Capital	Corporate Venture Capital	Accelerator or /	Accelerator or / Company Building	Company Building	Venture Clienting/ Merger & Acquisitions	Merger & Acquisition	

7.25 Value Co-Creation

Value co-creation is a strategic approach in business and innovation where companies collaborate with external stakeholders, such as customers, suppliers, and partners, to jointly produce a mutually valued outcome. This concept is rooted in the idea that customers can contribute significantly to the value creation process.

7.25.1 Understanding Value Co-Creation

- **Engagement of Stakeholders**: Involves actively engaging various stakeholders in the development, production, and marketing processes.
- **Shared Value Creation**: Focuses on creating value that is beneficial to both the company and its stakeholders.

7.25.2 Application in Business and Innovation

- Companies use co-creation to innovate products and services by incorporating customer feedback and ideas directly into the development process.

- Co-creation is often used in service design, where customer experience is paramount.

7.25.3 Examples of Value Co-Creation

1. **LEGO Ideas**: LEGO Ideas is a platform where fans submit and vote on new product ideas. Winning ideas are turned into new LEGO sets, with creators receiving recognition and a percentage of sales.

2. **Starbucks**: Starbucks has used co-creation by allowing customers to suggest and vote on ideas for new drinks, store designs, and services through their 'My Starbucks Idea' platform.

7.25.4 Challenges in Implementing Value Co-Creation

- **Managing Diverse Inputs**: Balancing and integrating inputs from various stakeholders can be complex.

- **Quality Control**: Ensuring that co-created products or services maintain a high standard.

- **Intellectual Property**: Navigating the challenges of IP when ideas are sourced from external contributors.

7.25.5 Best Practices for Value Co-Creation

- **Clear Communication**: Establish transparent communication channels with all participants.

- **Customer-Centric Approach**: Focus on understanding and meeting customer needs and expectations.

- **Feedback Loops**: Implement efficient feedback mechanisms to capture stakeholder inputs.

Value co-creation represents a shift from a company-centric view of value creation to a more collaborative approach. By engaging customers and other stakeholders in the creation process, companies can innovate more effectively and produce offerings that better meet market needs.

7.26 Messaging Map

Introduction to Messaging Maps A Messaging Map is a strategic communication tool used in marketing and business communication. It helps organizations articulate and organize their key messages in a coherent and consistent manner. This tool is essential for ensuring that all communication, both internal and external, aligns with the company's overall messaging strategy.

7.26.1 Core Elements of a Messaging Map

- **Value Proposition**: Clearly articulates the unique value the company or product offers.
- **Target Audience**: Identifies the different segments of the audience and tailors messages to each.
- **Key Messages**: Outlines the main points that need to be communicated to the audience.
- **Supporting Messages**: Provides additional information to back up the key messages.

7.26.2 Application in Business Communication

- **Product Launches**: Ensures consistent messaging across all channels during a product launch.
- **Branding Campaigns**: Helps maintain a consistent brand voice across various media and platforms.
- **Crisis Communication**: Aids in delivering clear and unified messages during a crisis.

7.26.3 Examples of Messaging Maps

1. **Technology Product Launch**: A tech company might use a messaging map to highlight a new product's innovative features, targeting different messages to tech enthusiasts, potential business users, and general consumers.
2. **Healthcare Campaign**: A healthcare provider could use a messaging map to communicate the benefits of a new wellness program, tailoring messages for patients, healthcare professionals, and insurance providers.

7.26.4 Challenges in Developing Messaging Maps
- **Consistency**: Maintaining a consistent message across all channels and touchpoints.
- **Relevance**: Ensuring messages are relevant and resonate with the target audience.
- **Simplicity**: Keeping messages clear and straightforward while conveying all necessary information.

7.26.5 Best Practices for Creating Effective Messaging Maps
- **Audience Understanding**: Deeply understand your audience to tailor messages effectively.
- **Alignment with Business Goals**: Ensure that all messages align with the overall business and marketing objectives.
- **Flexibility**: Allow for some flexibility in messaging to adapt to different contexts and media.

Messaging Maps are vital tools for ensuring consistent and effective communication in various business contexts. By clearly defining and organizing key messages, companies can communicate more effectively with their target audiences and achieve their communication objectives.

7.27 Customer Journey Mapping

Customer Journey Mapping is a strategic approach to understanding and visualizing the customer's experience with a product or service. This technique involves creating a detailed map of every touchpoint and interaction a customer has with a brand, offering insights into their needs, motivations, and pain points.

7.27.1 The Process of Customer Journey Mapping
1. **Identify Customer Personas**: Start by defining the different types of customers who use the product or service.
2. **Map Touchpoints**: Identify all the points where customers interact with the brand, from initial awareness to post-purchase.
3. **Analyze Customer Experiences**: Explore the customer's thoughts, feelings, and actions at each touchpoint.

4. **Identify Pain Points and Opportunities**: Look for areas where customers face challenges or where there are opportunities for improvement.

7.27.2 Applications of Customer Journey Mapping

- **Product and Service Design**: Improving design based on customer interaction and feedback.
- **Marketing Strategy**: Tailoring marketing efforts to align with customer experiences and expectations.
- **Customer Experience Enhancement**: Identifying ways to improve the overall customer experience.

7.27.3 Benefits of Customer Journey Mapping

- **Enhanced Customer Understanding**: Provides a deep understanding of customer behaviors and preferences.
- **Identifies Improvement Areas**: Highlights areas where changes or improvements can significantly impact customer satisfaction.
- **Fosters Cross-Functional Collaboration**: Encourages different departments to work together towards a common goal of improving the customer experience.

7.27.4 Examples of Customer Journey Mapping in Action

1. **E-commerce Platforms**: Mapping the journey of online shoppers to identify friction points in the browsing, selection, checkout, and delivery processes.
2. **Banking Services**: Understanding the customer experience from opening an account to using various banking services to improve customer service and product offerings.

7.27.5 Challenges in Customer Journey Mapping

- **Data Collection**: Gathering comprehensive and accurate data across all touchpoints can be challenging.
- **Complexity of Journeys**: Customer journeys can be complex and varied, making them difficult to map accurately.
- **Dynamic Customer Behaviors**: Customer preferences and behaviors can change, requiring continuous updates to the journey maps.

7.27.6 Best Practices for Effective Customer Journey Mapping

- **Customer-Centric Focus**: Always keep the customer's perspective at the center of the mapping process.

- **Regular Updates**: Update journey maps regularly to reflect changes in customer behavior and market dynamics.

- **Stakeholder Involvement**: Involve stakeholders from across the organization to provide a complete view of the customer journey.

Customer Journey Mapping is an invaluable tool in the ideation process, helping businesses to empathize with their customers and design products, services, and experiences that truly meet their needs. By visualizing the customer's journey, organizations can identify key areas for innovation and improvement, leading to enhanced customer satisfaction and loyalty.

7.28 EMPATHY MAPS IN INNOVATION

Empathy Maps are a user-centered design tool that helps innovators deeply understand their target users. They visualize user attitudes and behaviors, providing insights into users' needs and wants. This tool is crucial in ensuring that innovations are not just technically feasible but also human-centered and relevant to the users' experiences.

7.28.1 Understanding Empathy Maps

An Empathy Map typically consists of four quadrants:

1. **Says**: What the user says about the product or service.
2. **Thinks**: What the user is thinking while using the product.
3. **Does**: The actions the user takes in relation to the product.
4. **Feels**: The emotions the user experiences.

7.28.2 Application in Innovation

- **Product Development**: Used to design products that truly resonate with users' needs and preferences.

- **Customer Experience Design**: Helps in understanding the customer journey and enhancing their overall experience.

- **Marketing Strategy**: Assists in creating targeted marketing strategies that speak to users' emotions and needs.

7.28.3 Benefits of Empathy Maps
- **Deep User Understanding**: Offers a comprehensive understanding of the user beyond basic demographics.
- **Enhanced User Experience**: Leads to innovations that are more aligned with what users want and need.
- **Effective Communication**: Helps teams communicate about users in a more nuanced and empathetic way.

7.28.4 Examples of Empathy Maps in Action
1. **Healthcare App Development**: A healthcare company might use empathy maps to understand patients' experiences, fears, and needs while managing their health, leading to more patient-friendly app features.
2. **Retail Customer Experience**: A retailer could use empathy maps to understand the shopping experience from a customer's perspective, leading to improved store layout and customer service strategies.

7.28.5 Challenges in Creating Empathy Maps
- **Accurate Data Collection**: Gathering authentic and unbiased information about what users say, think, do, and feel can be challenging.
- **Subjectivity**: There's a risk of projecting one's own assumptions onto the map, rather than truly representing the user's perspective.
- **Integration into Processes**: Effectively integrating empathy maps into the overall innovation and design process.

7.28.6 Best Practices for Using Empathy Maps
- **User Engagement**: Directly engage with users through interviews or observations to gather authentic insights.
- **Regular Updates**: Update empathy maps regularly to reflect changes in user behavior or market trends.

- **Cross-Functional Collaboration**: Use empathy maps as a collaborative tool across different teams to ensure a shared understanding of the user.

Empathy Maps are a vital tool in the innovation process, ensuring that user perspectives are central to the development of products, services, and experiences. By providing a deep understanding of users, empathy maps enable innovators to create solutions that are not only technically sound but also deeply resonant with their target audience.

7.29 THE KANO MODEL IN INNOVATION

The Kano Model, developed by Professor Noriaki Kano in the 1980s, is a theory for product development and customer satisfaction. It categorizes customer preferences into five categories and helps innovators understand and prioritize features based on customer perceptions and potential impact on satisfaction.

7.29.1 Understanding the Kano Model Categories

1. **Basic Needs**: Features that customers expect by default. Their absence causes dissatisfaction.

2. **Performance Needs**: Features that increase customer satisfaction in proportion to their level of functionality.

3. **Excitement Needs**: Unexpected features that can delight customers and positively influence satisfaction.

4. **Indifferent Needs**: Features to which customers are neutral.

5. **Reverse Needs**: Features that can cause dissatisfaction if present.

7.29.2 Application in Innovation

- **Product Design and Development**: Identifying and incorporating features that align with customer expectations and desires.

- **Customer Experience Strategy**: Enhancing the customer experience by focusing on elements that significantly impact satisfaction.

- **Market Differentiation**: Identifying excitement needs can provide a competitive edge.

7.29.3 Benefits of Using the Kano Model

- **Focused Innovation**: Helps prioritize features and innovations that will have the most significant impact on customer satisfaction.
- **Balanced Product Features**: Ensures a balance between basic, performance, and excitement features.
- **Enhanced Customer Understanding**: Provides insights into the different levels of customer needs and preferences.

7.29.4 Examples of the Kano Model in Practice

1. **Smartphones**: Basic needs might include reliability and battery life, performance needs could be camera quality, and excitement needs might be innovative features like facial recognition or augmented reality.
2. **Automotive Industry**: Basic needs are safety and reliability, performance needs include fuel efficiency, and excitement needs could be advanced driver-assistance systems.

7.29.5 Challenges in Applying the Kano Model

- **Evolving Customer Expectations**: Customer expectations can shift over time, turning excitement needs into basic needs.
- **Subjective Interpretation**: Determining which features fall into which category can be subjective and vary among different customer segments.
- **Resource Allocation**: Balancing resources to meet all types of needs effectively.

7.29.6 Best Practices for Implementing the Kano Model

- **Regular Customer Feedback**: Regularly gather and analyze customer feedback to understand their evolving needs.
- **Dynamic Approach**: Revisit the Kano analysis periodically to reflect changes in the market and customer expectations.
- **Cross-Functional Collaboration**: Collaborate across departments to ensure a comprehensive understanding of customer needs.

The Kano Model offers a strategic approach to understanding customer satisfaction and can guide innovators in creating products that not only meet but exceed customer expectations. By effectively applying this model, businesses can ensure that their innovations are customer-centric and market-relevant.

7.30 User Personas or Customer Personas

Personas are fictional characters created to represent different user types within a targeted demographic, attitude, and behavior set. In the context of innovation, personas are used to humanize the target audience, helping innovators and designers to understand and cater to the specific needs and desires of different user groups.

7.30.1 Creating Personas for Innovation

- **Data Collection**: Gather data through market research, interviews, surveys, and observation.
- **Segmentation**: Identify common patterns and themes in the data to segment the audience.
- **Character Creation**: Develop detailed profiles for each persona, including demographics, behaviors, needs, goals, and pain points.
- **Usage**: Use these personas to guide decision-making in the innovation process.

7.30.2 Applications of Personas in Innovation

- **Product Development**: Tailoring product features and designs to meet the specific needs of different user groups.
- **Marketing Strategy**: Developing targeted marketing campaigns that resonate with different personas.
- **Customer Experience Design**: Creating and enhancing customer experiences based on the preferences and behaviors of the personas.

7.30.3 Benefits of Using Personas

- **Empathy and Understanding**: Fosters empathy and a deeper understanding of the target audience.

- **Focused Innovation**: Helps in focusing innovation efforts on creating solutions that truly meet user needs.

- **Better Communication**: Aids in communicating the target audience's characteristics and needs across the team or organization.

7.30.4 Examples of Personas in Innovation

1. **Tech Company**: A tech company might create personas like 'Tech-Savvy Teenager', 'Busy Professional', and 'Retiree' to guide the development of a new app, ensuring it meets the varying needs and preferences of these groups.

2. **Healthcare Provider**: For a new healthcare app, personas such as 'Chronic Patient', 'Fitness Enthusiast', and 'Caregiver' can help in tailoring features like appointment scheduling, fitness tracking, and patient care management.

7.30.5 Challenges in Using Personas

- **Accuracy**: Ensuring that personas accurately reflect the target audience can be challenging, requiring ongoing updates and validation.

- **Overgeneralization**: There's a risk of oversimplifying or stereotyping user groups.

- **Integration into Processes**: Effectively integrating personas into the entire innovation process can be difficult.

7.30.6 Best Practices for Effective Use of Personas

- **Realistic and Detailed Profiles**: Develop detailed and realistic personas based on actual data.

- **Regular Updates**: Update personas regularly to reflect changes in the target audience or market.

- **Cross-Functional Use**: Encourage the use of personas across different departments for a unified understanding of the target audience.

Personas are a powerful tool in the innovation process, providing a human-centered approach to understanding and meeting the needs of different user groups. By creating and utilizing detailed personas, innovators can ensure that their products, services, and experiences are relevant, appealing, and effective for their intended audiences.

7.31 Morphological Analysis in Innovation

Morphological Analysis (MA) is a method developed by Fritz Zwicky in the 1960s for exploring all possible solutions to a multi-dimensional, non-quantified problem complex. In the context of innovation, it is a technique used to generate new ideas and product concepts by examining the relationships between different dimensions or attributes of a problem.

7.31.1 Understanding Morphological Analysis

MA involves breaking down a problem into its key components or dimensions and then systematically examining the possible options for each component. The goal is to explore a wide range of combinations of these components, leading to innovative solutions or product ideas.

7.31.2 The Process of Morphological Analysis

1. **Identify the Problem Dimensions**: Break down the problem into key dimensions or attributes.

2. **Generate Options for Each Dimension**: List all possible options or variations for each dimension.

3. **Create a Morphological Box**: A grid or matrix (Zwicky Box) is used to map out the dimensions and their respective options.

4. **Analyze Combinations**: Explore different combinations of options to identify innovative solutions.

7.31.3 Applications of Morphological Analysis in Innovation

- **Product Design**: Developing new product concepts by exploring various combinations of features.

- **Service Innovation**: Creating new service offerings by combining different service elements in novel ways.

- **Problem-Solving**: Addressing complex problems that require creative solutions.

7.31.4 Benefits of Morphological Analysis

- **Comprehensive Idea Generation**: Ensures a thorough exploration of potential solutions.

- **Breaks Down Complex Problems**: Simplifies complex problems by examining them in smaller, more manageable parts.

- **Promotes Creative Thinking**: Encourages thinking outside the box and exploring unconventional solutions.

7.31.5 Examples of Morphological Analysis in Action

1. **Automotive Design**: A car manufacturer uses MA to explore different combinations of powertrains, body styles, and features, leading to the creation of a new car model.

2. **Software Development**: A software company applies MA to combine various functionalities, user interfaces, and technologies, resulting in an innovative software product.

7.31.6 Challenges in Applying Morphological Analysis

- **Overwhelming Options**: The number of potential combinations can be vast and overwhelming.

- **Resource Intensive**: Analyzing all possible combinations requires significant time and resources.

- **Practicality and Feasibility**: Not all combinations generated through MA may be practical or feasible.

7.31.7 Best Practices for Effective Morphological Analysis

- **Focused Scope**: Limit the number of dimensions and options to a manageable size.

- **Diverse Perspectives**: Involve a diverse group of people in the MA process to bring in different viewpoints.

- **Iterative Process**: Use MA as an iterative process, refining and narrowing down options as you progress.

Morphological Analysis is a powerful tool for innovation, allowing for a systematic exploration of a wide range of possibilities. By breaking down complex problems and creatively recombining different elements, it paves the way for groundbreaking solutions and products.

7.32 Six Thinking Hats in Innovation

The Six Thinking Hats, a concept developed by Edward de Bono, is a tool for group discussion and individual thinking that involves six colored hats, each representing a different style of thinking. In innovation, this methodology facilitates diverse perspectives, encourages creativity, and streamlines decision-making processes.

7.32.1 Understanding the Six Hats

1. **White Hat (Information)**: Focuses on available data and information, looking at what is known and needed.

2. **Red Hat (Emotions)**: Encourages the expression of emotions and feelings without justification.

3. **Black Hat (Judgment)**: Cautious and critical thinking to identify barriers or risks.

4. **Yellow Hat (Optimism)**: Positive, speculative thinking to explore benefits and value.

5. **Green Hat (Creativity)**: Creative thinking to generate new ideas and alternatives.

6. **Blue Hat (Process Control)**: Manages the thinking process and ensures each hat is utilized effectively.

7.32.2 Application in Innovation

- **Idea Generation and Evaluation**: Using different hats to explore and evaluate ideas from multiple perspectives.

- **Problem-Solving**: Addressing complex problems by systematically applying each thinking style.

- **Team Collaboration**: Facilitating effective and balanced team discussions and brainstorming sessions.

7.32.3 Benefits of Using Six Thinking Hats

- **Diverse Perspectives**: Ensures consideration of different viewpoints and approaches.

- **Structured Thinking**: Provides a structured way to tackle problems and explore ideas.

- **Reduced Conflict**: Allows for open expression of emotions and concerns in a controlled environment.

7.32.4 Examples of Six Thinking Hats in Innovation

1. **Product Development Team**: A team developing a new product might use the hats to explore market needs (white), emotional appeal (red), potential risks (black), advantages (yellow), innovative features (green), and organize the development process (blue).

2. **Marketing Strategy Session**: While developing a marketing strategy, the team employs different hats to analyze market data (white), gauge customer reactions (red), identify possible challenges (black), foresee campaign success (yellow), brainstorm creative strategies (green), and plan the campaign (blue).

7.32.5 Challenges in Implementing Six Thinking Hats

- **Participant Buy-In**: Some team members might find it challenging to adopt different thinking styles.

- **Balancing the Hats**: Ensuring that each hat is given adequate time and consideration.

- **Facilitation**: Requires a skilled facilitator to guide the process and ensure productive discussions.

7.32.6 Best Practices for Effective Use of Six Thinking Hats

- **Clear Understanding of Each Hat**: Ensure that all participants understand the role and purpose of each hat.

- **Equal Participation**: Encourage all members to contribute under each hat.

- **Flexible Use**: Adapt the use of the hats to fit the context and needs of the discussion.

The Six Thinking Hats is an effective tool for driving innovation by enabling teams to explore ideas and problems from different angles. By fostering a structured yet creative and holistic approach to thinking, this method enhances the quality of decision-making and idea generation.

www.ingramcontent.com/pod-product-compliance
Lightning Source LLC
Chambersburg PA
CBHW052200220526
45471CB00004B/1752